access to history

themes

END OF EMPIRES: EUROPEAN DECOLONISATION 1919–80

access to history

themes

END OF EMPIRES: EUROPEAN DECOLONISATION 1919–80

Gary Thorn

Hodder & Stoughton

A MEMBER OF THE HODDER HEADLINE GROUP

For all my students, past and present, who told me their decolonisation stories.

Acknowledgements

My thanks are due to the following people for their help: Dr. Peter Neville, for first suggesting the project; Dr. Bernard Waites, for sharing his ideas with me at an early stage; Professor Patrick Chabal, for commenting on the Portuguese material; Tony Davis, for the English; Pamela Moir, for the French; Jonathan Guy, for Library support; and Dr. Bob Pearce, for being the model editor, academically meticulous but always encouraging. The responsibility for the History is entirely mine.

The publishers would like to thank the following individuals, institutions and companies for permission to use copyright illustrations in this volume:

Hulton-Deutsch Collection/CORBIS pages 43, 73; Cummings, *Daily Express*, Centre for the Study of Cartoons and Caricature, University of Kent, Canterbury, page 49; Society for Cooperation in Russian & Soviet Studies, page 49; Bettmann/CORBIS pages 53, 115; *Purnell's History of the Twentieth Century*, Vol. 5 pages 94, 96.

The publishers would like to thank the following for permission to reproduce material in this volume: Blackwell Publishers Ltd/Polity Press for an extract from *Decolonization: The Fall of the European Empires* by M.E. Chamberlain, Blackwell Publishers Ltd/Polity Press, 1985; Cambridge University Press for extracts from *The Invention of Tradition* edited by E.J. Hobsbawm and T.O. Ranger,1983, and *British Imperialism 1750–1970* by Simon C. Smith,1998; Patrick Chabal for extracts from *Amilcar Cabral: Revolutionary Leadership and People's War*, Cambridge University Press, 1983; HarperCollins Publishers Ltd for extracts from *The Rise and Fall of the Great Powers: Economic Change and Military Conflict from 1500 to 2000* by Paul Kennedy, Fontana, 1989, and *Harold Wilson* by Ben Pimlott, 1992; Hodder & Stoughton Educational for extracts from *France 1914–69 The Three Republics* by Peter Neville, 1995; *The Independent*/Syndication for an extract from 'Mobutu takes the money and runs to a safe haven' by Mary Braid in *The Independent*, 17 May 1997; Little Brown for extracts from *The Last Great Frenchman: A Life of General de Gaulle* by Charles Williams, Abacus, 1993; Lynne Rienner Publishers for extracts from *The World Since 1945: A History of International Relations* by Wayne C. McWilliams and Harry Piotrowski, 4th edition, Lynne Rienner, 1997; Palgrave for extracts from *France and Decolonisation, 1900–1960* by Raymond F. Betts, Macmillan, 1991; *Britain and Decolonisation: The Retreat from Empire in the Post-War World* by John Darwin, Macmillan, 1988; *European Decolonisation 1918-80: An Introductory Survey* by R.F. Holland, Macmillan, 1985; *A History of the West Indies* by J.H. Parry and Philip Sherlock, Macmillan, 1971; and *Europe and the Third World: From Colonialism to Decolonisation, c.1500–1998* by Bernard Waites, Macmillan, 1999; Pearson Education Ltd for extracts from *British Imperialism: Crisis and Deconstruction 1914-1990* by P.J. Cain and A.G. Hopkins, Longman, 1993, and *Decolonization in Africa* by J.D. Hargreaves, Longman, 1988; Penguin Books Ltd for extracts from pages 214, 345 of *Age of Extremes: The Short Twentieth Century 1914–91* by E.J. Hobsbawm, Michael Joseph, 1994, © E.J. Hobsbawm 1994, and page 88 of *The World Since 1945* by T.E. Vadney, Penguin Books, 1987, © T.E. Vadney 1987, 1992; Routledge for extracts from *Decolonization* by Raymond Betts, Routledge, 1998, and *Colonization: A Global History* by Marc Ferro, Routledge, 1997; Sage Publications Ltd for extracts from 'Imperial Hangovers: Belgium – The Economics of Decolonization' by Jean-Philippe Peemans in *Journal of Contemporary History*, vol.15, Sage, 1980; Yale University Press for extracts from *Gandhi: Prisoner of Hope* by Judith M. Brown, *Decolonization and African Independence: The Transfers of Power, 1960–1980*, edited by Prosser Gifford and William Roger Louis,1988, and *The African Colonial State in Comparative Respect* by Crawford Young,1997.

Every effort has been made to trace and acknowledge ownership of copyright. The publishers will be glad to make suitable arrangements with any copyright holders whom it has not been possible to contact.

Orders: please contact Bookpoint Ltd, 78 Milton Park, Abingdon, Oxon OX14 4TD. Telephone (44) 01235 827720, Fax: (44) 01235 400454. Lines are open from 9.00–6.00, Monday to Saturday, with a 24 hour message answering service. Email address: orders@bookpoint.co.uk

British Library Cataloguing in Publication Data
A catalogue record for this title is available from the British Library

ISBN 0 340 73044 7

First published 2000
Impression number   10 9 8 7 6 5 4 3 2 1
Year   2005 2004 2003 2002 2001

Cover photo from Popperfoto
Typeset by Fakenham Photosetting Limited, Fakenham, Norfolk.
Printed in Great Britain for Hodder & Stoughton Educational, a division of Hodder Headline Plc, 338 Euston Road, London NW1 3BH by Redwood Books Ltd.

Contents

Preface

The original *Access to History* series was conceived as a collection of sets of books covering popular chronological periods in British history, together with the histories of other countries, such as France, Germany, Russia and the USA. This arrangement complemented the way in which history has traditionally been taught in sixth forms, colleges and universities. In recent years, however, other ways of dividing up the past have become increasingly popular. In particular, there has been a greater emphasis on studying relatively brief periods in considerable detail and on comparing similar historical phenomena in different countries. These developments have generated a demand for appropriate learning materials, and, in response, two new 'strands' have been added to the main series – *In Depth* and *Themes*. The new volumes build directly on the features that have made *Access to History* so popular.

To the general reader

Access books have been specifically designed to meet the needs of examination students, but they also have much to offer the general reader. The authors are committed to the belief that good history must not only be accurate, up-to-date and scholarly, but also clearly and attractively written. The main body of the text (excluding the Study Guide sections) should therefore form a readable and engaging survey of a topic. Moreover, each author has aimed not merely to provide as clear an explanation as possible of what happened in the past but also to stimulate readers and to challenge them into thinking for themselves about the past and its significance. Thus, although no prior knowledge is expected from the reader, he or she is treated as an intelligent and thinking person throughout. The author tends to share ideas and explore possibilities, instead of delivering so-called 'historical truths' from on high.

To the student reader

It is intended that *Access* books should be used by students studying history at a higher level. Its volumes are all designed to be working texts, which should be reasonably clear on a first reading but which will benefit from re-reading and close study.

To be an effective and successful student, you need to budget your time wisely. Hence you should think carefully about how important the material in a particular book is for you. If you simply need to acquire a general grasp of a topic, the following approach will probably be effective:

1. Read Chapter 1, which should give you an overview of the whole book, and think about its contents.
2. Skim through Chapter 2, paying particular attention to the 'Points to

Consider' box and to the 'Key Issue' highlighted at the start of each section. Decide if you need to read the whole chapter.
3. If you do, read the chapter, stopping at the end of every sub-division of the text to make notes.
4. Repeat stage 2 (and stage 3 where appropriate) for the other chapters.

If, however, your course demands a detailed knowledge of the contents of the book, you will need to be correspondingly more thorough. There is no perfect way of studying, and it is particularly worthwhile experimenting with different styles of note-making to find the one that best suits you. Nevertheless the following plan of action is worth trying:

1. Read a whole chapter quickly, preferably at one sitting. Avoid the temptation – which may be very great – to make notes at this stage.
2. Study the diagram at the end of the chapter, ensuring that you understand the general 'shape' of what you have read.
3. Re-read the chapter more slowly, this time taking notes. You may well be amazed at how much more intelligible and straightforward the material seems on a second reading – and your notes will be correspondingly more useful to you when you have to write an essay or revise for an exam. In the long run, reading a chapter twice can, in fact, often save time. Be sure to make your notes in a clear, orderly fashion, and spread them out so that, if necessary, you can later add extra information.
4. The Study Guide sections will be particularly valuable for those taking AS level, A level and Higher. Read the advice on essay questions, and do tackle the specimen titles. (Remember that if learning is to be effective, it must be active. No one – alas – has yet devised any substitute for real effort. It is up to you to make up your own mind on the key issues in any topic.)
5. Attempt the source-based questions. The guidance on tackling these exercises is well worth reading and thinking about.

When you have finished the main chapters, go through the 'Further Reading' section. Remember that no single book can ever do more than introduce a topic, and it is to be hoped that, time permitting, you will want to read more widely. If *Access* books help you to discover just how diverse and fascinating the human past can be, the series will have succeeded in its aim – and you will experience that enthusiasm for the subject which, along with efficient learning, is the hallmark of the best students.

Robert Pearce

1 Introduction: Understanding Decolonisation

POINTS TO CONSIDER

This first chapter introduces you to the historical meaning of decolonisation and to the main problems historians encounter when studying it. It discusses how they go about solving these problems. You should pay particular attention to the historiographical debate as outlined in the section on models. It then examines the background to decolonisation in the history of European imperialism and provides an outline chronology of how decolonisation developed. Finally, it offers advice on how to link all this to the forthcoming chapters.

KEY DATES

1415	Portuguese took Ceuta in North Africa, beginning the age of European colonisation
1763	British established dominance over French interests in India
1830	Algeria became a French colony: beginning of modern French colonialism
1882	British occupation of Egypt began 'The New Imperialism' in Africa
1914–18	First World War caused losses of empire for some, gains for others
1930s	Economic depression placed new strains upon empires
1939–45	Second World War destroyed some empires, weakened the survivors, caused rise of superpowers and Cold War
1947	Indian independence
1954	French defeated in Indo-China; Indonesian independence from the Dutch
1957–65	Main period of British decolonisation
1956–62	Main period of French decolonisation
1960	Belgium withdrew from the Congo
1974	Portuguese Revolution; independence for Guinea-Bissau and Cape Verde
1975	Independence for Angola and Mozambique
1980	Independence for Zimbabwe, last major decolonisation in Africa

1 Problems of Studying Decolonisation

KEY ISSUE Why is decolonisation a difficult historical problem?

a) Definition

If you were to tell somebody who was not studying history that you had just begun to read a book about decolonisation you might be greeted with a momentary look of puzzled silence. It is a long word – historians cannot even agree how to spell it – and its meaning is often vague to the ordinary person. This unfamiliarity might seem surprising, for the evidence of decolonisation is all around us in multi-cultural societies. White, black and Asian people mix with each other in early twenty-first century Europe in almost all walks of life. But it was not always so, and this book is about the changing relationships between such people across continents through the twentieth century.

One reason for poor understanding of decolonisation is that many people have only partial knowledge of it. They might, for example, take it to mean immigration. Its causes, rooted in relationships established during colonial rule, might be unknown to them, seemingly hidden in the history of places thousands of miles away. A major purpose of a book like this is to unlock that history. Its aim is to outline the causes, effects, similarities and differences of some of the most important examples of decolonisation, and to assess their impact upon the modern world.

So, without further delay, let us grapple with the problem of defining exactly what decolonisation means. It is a relatively new word in the English language. The historian John Hargreaves claims that it did not enter into the best dictionaries and encyclopaedias until the mid-1970s. I can confirm this from my own 1970 reprint of the *Concise Oxford Dictionary* (first edition 1964) where the word does not appear. However, dictionaries are of limited use as historical sources. Hargreaves knows this and has searched official documents to find an earliest reference from 1932. It was certainly in common use by historians by the 1960s. For example, from the works listed in the bibliography of this book, the earliest publication to have the word in the title is Henri Grimal's *Decolonization: the British, French, Dutch and Belgian Empires 1919–63*, first published in France in 1963.

It is interesting that historians rarely bother defining the term, and you will note that I am still procrastinating! For the purposes of this book, it means the historical process by which the European powers who had established empires in the non-European world ceased to rule those regions. I emphasise *historical* process because it is largely a term invented by historians, and the peoples who experienced the process might choose not to use it. For example, it has to be admitted that it is a term more fitting the perspective of decolonisers than decolonised. The former are inclined to see what was happening as the reversal of a process that they had initiated, namely colonisation. They might even talk about the 'retreat from empire', as some who regret it still do. The decolonised would be more inclined to see themselves as taking the initiative, through nationalist movements of liberation to achieve *independence* rather than decolonisation. Neither would my definition satisfy an historian like Marc Ferro[1]. His decolonisations would include withdrawal from European territories, as the Russians did from the Baltic states after 1991. Whereas such extended definitions can be of great use, I am not going to extend mine to include a notion of a 'Soviet empire'.

Neither does the problem of definition end there. Decolonisation's roots lie in colonisation, or in imperialism, if you prefer. Most historians distinguish between imperialism and colonisation. If imperialism was the process of creating empires, colonisation refers only to those parts that were actually settled in by the people of the imperialist power. Some historians use the terms 'informal' and 'formal' empire to describe these conditions. Therefore, colonisation is a specific variant of imperialism. This is a fine distinction and you will notice these terms used interchangeably throughout this book. *Decolonisation* is used to describe European withdrawal from either situation. Fortunately, we never use the term deimperialism!

b) Conceptual Accuracy

Differences in experience between the decolonised areas are often so great that they seem to outweigh the similarities. Raymond Betts thinks differences so great that we cannot call it a single process of history at all, just a set of similar experiences.[2] How much does the history of India really have in common with that of Vietnam, for example, apart from the fact they were both once ruled over by (different) European powers? This raises the question of the overall accuracy of the concept of decolonisation. We have already noted Ferro's stretching of it to include 'Soviet decolonisation' after 1991.

c) Scope and Selection

European empires covered a large part of the globe by the beginning of the twentieth century. Studying their disintegration is, therefore, a global problem. Comprehensive histories of decolonisation, such as Marc Ferro's ambitious enterprise referred to above, amount to the writing of world history. As a short work, this book makes no pretence at being comprehensive. It is necessarily selective in its treatment. It presents representative examples from the history of the five main empires that decolonised: Britain, France, the Netherlands, Belgium and Portugal. More attention is paid to those decolonisations that resulted in violence and war. Some readers, I fear, may be disappointed by this, particularly Afro-Caribbean ones. I hope they will still read on.

d) Periodisation

It is common to discuss decolonisation as a post-Second World War phenomenon, but this is open to the criticism that the war was not the main cause of decolonisation. A nationalist, wishing to emphasise the role of 'liberation movements', would point to the fact that nationalists had been trying to get rid of European rule for far longer than that. In this view a post-1945 periodisation would be seen as a European (or Eurocentric) perspective. This is not an either/or choice of approach, but a question of balance. The one adopted in this book is to locate the causes of decolonisation over the longer term, while explaining its precise timing through changing post-war international relations. The Second World War is seen as an important accelerator of change. Pre-1945 decolonisations, such as Egypt (1922) and Iraq (1932) still need to be accounted for.

e) Continuity and change

Decolonisation is full of paradoxes, to confuse and test the student of its history. This has been cleverly presented by H.L. Wesseling: 'Decolonisation has finished. It definitely belongs to the past. Yet somehow it has refused to become history.'[3] The evidence for this is not hard to find as one walks any urban street or tunes in to world television news. Africa and Asia are unavoidably present in multicultural Europe. The converse is, however, less true. How many white people had Angolan peasants seen before Princess Diana arrived in that famous white helmet protecting her from *perigo* (danger)? Perhaps an aid worker or two. The evidence that decolonisation has not ended Third World poverty is before our eyes in this age of global communications. While the developed world contemplates the prospect of 'e universities' it is salutary to reflect on their lack of meaning for a malnourished Angolan child who would love to walk to school if only there was one to go to, and she still had legs (Angola's wars have resulted in the world's highest amputation rate). If she were able to get 'netted-up' she might browse the writings of a school of history that explains the continuity of post-colonial poverty by the theory of 'neo-colonialism' (that is '... situations in which underdeveloped nations achieved political independence but remained economically dependent upon the West'[4]). It sits alongside other ideas that we shall meet in forthcoming chapters, such as those drawn from post-colonial studies, which are concerned with the broad cultural consequences of decolonisation.

f) Moral judgement

Decolonisation history raises questions of moral judgement that are difficult to avoid. This is because European colonisation was founded upon inequality, exploitation, and even genocide inflicted by white upon non-white peoples. There is nothing funny about this, but the oppressed have a history of using humour both to resist and keep up morale. A much-told African joke runs as follows. 'When the white man came to Africa, *we* had the land and he had the bibles. He said, let us close our eyes and pray. When we opened them again, *he* had the land and we had the bibles!' The joke is short yet profound. Colonialism, it says, was theft, aided and abetted by the Christian religion.

But history is not that simple. Historians of slavery have pointed out that blacks enslaved other blacks before whites began to do so. One school of historians explains imperialism by arguing that the developed 'core' of capitalist powers collaborated with elites in the 'periphery' of the undeveloped world. After decolonisation these post-colonial elites reproduced patterns of exploitation learned from Europeans. As they did so, they continued to accommodate European influence informally through 'neo-colonialism'. Has decolonisation, therefore, not been 'freedom' at all but merely the exchange of one system of subjugation for another? In trying to answer such questions the historian's first task is to explain, not to judge. Sometimes, however, the evidence makes moral judgement difficult to avoid, in the way that it is for those who study the Holocaust.

2 Models for Interpreting the History of Decolonisation

> **KEY ISSUE** What ideas have historians produced to try to make our understanding of decolonisation clearer?

a) Why use models?

Decolonisation history, then, is full of problems. We have to define our terms carefully, justify our use of them, select our evidence appropriately, periodise accurately, calculate the balance of change against continuity, and distinguish between historical and moral judgement. No wonder historians flinch when others say that what they do is easy because it is just about learning the facts! At such moments they might feel like reaching for an aspirin, but sensibly they usually settle for a model instead.

I once had a senior colleague who felt no such need. When asked which textbooks he used to teach post-1945 history he replied, 'None. I can remember it all.' His reply should strike a warning for contemporary historians. Living through an historical period does not enable us to be certain about our interpretations. In fact, certainty is sometimes made more difficult by the withholding of evidence. For example, the British government imposes a 30-year rule on the use of certain types of sensitive official papers. After 1974, Portuguese governments withheld similarly sensitive and incriminating material to protect those who served the dictatorship and were still alive. It is not surprising that historians disagree when they try to evaluate the causes of decolonisation. They produce interpretations or models.

b) Models

i) The decline of the metropole

There are two versions of this. The first argues that decolonisation took place because the colonial power (metropole) declined economically and became too weak to hold on to empire. This applies best to the decline of the Portuguese dictatorship, described in chapter 5. The second argues that metropoles withdrew because they took rational decisions that it was no longer in their economic or political interests to stay. British and Belgian decolonisations would be the best examples of this. Both versions locate the central cause of decolonisation firmly within the decolonising power. It is, therefore, a Eurocentric interpretation (i.e. an interpretation centred on Europe).

ii) The Bipolar World of the Superpowers

The Second World War produced a fundamental re-distribution of world power in favour of the USA and the USSR. It created a 'bipolar world'[5] (a world with two centres of power). After 1945 the two superpowers marginalised the colonial powers. The old type of imperialism, involving physical occupation and economic protection, did not fit the free market principles of the Americans who wanted access to world markets. Later this also enabled relocation of production in the Third World. For their part, the USSR responded to American 'neo-colonialism', as they defined it, by creating their own economic bloc. This consisted of the Eastern European states, plus other communist ones such as Cuba, North Vietnam and North Korea, although relations with China were difficult.

Paul Kennedy's model places decolonisation within a broader thesis about the reasons for the decline of great powers. For him, great powers, like the decolonising ones of the twentieth century, decline once they over-extend themselves. The colonial powers had reached this point by 1945. They no longer possessed the resources to hold on to what they had. It is similar to the first version of the decline of the metropole model, except that it places decolonisation within a combination of historical forces. As Kennedy puts it: 'What was happening, in fact, was that one major trend in twentieth-century power politics, the rise of the superpowers, was beginning to interact with another, newer trend – the political fragmentation of the globe.'[6] This is less of a Eurocentric model because it gives some weight to the rise of the Third World, as well as the USA. The fulcrum of change is located within shifts in international relations.

iii) The rise of nationalism

In contrast to the two models above, this one locates the prime cause of decolonisation within Asian and African nationalism. The colonisers were expelled. It was popular with historians who sympathised with such movements in the 1960s. Arguments for it can be found in the numerous autobiographies of the nationalist leaders celebrating their achievements in establishing new, independent states. The subsequent failure of many of these states to genuinely liberate all its peoples lost the thesis some credibility. Native elites merely seemed to replace colonial ones.

iv) Post-colonial theory: 'decolonising the mind'

The phrase quoted above is that of the Kenyan intellectual Ngugi wa Thiong'o who argues that the colonised are doubly alienated. The 'real' problems of economic and political oppression are more conspicuous than the other one of cultural domination.

As Ferro reminds us, the decolonised deserve a history of their own. In his cinematic analogy, they should not be relegated to the role of extras in the white man's film. The decolonised can be cast a leading role; yet, as long as the white man retains direction, he (the white man) is still open to the criticism that he is adopting a 'rose-coloured view', because as a European he is retaining '... one last privilege: that of painting its own misdeeds in dark colours and evaluating them on its own terms.'[7]

These arguments draw upon the work of historians of post-colonialism who use discourse theory to understand the effects of decolonisation. Put simply, they argue that we only understand the world through language (or discourse), therefore it is very powerful. This includes the language we use to interpret the past, for example in books, lectures or films. We are all brought up in different languages, the structures of which carry values as well as meanings. But all languages do not have equal power. For example, European ones like English, French or Portuguese are widely used and more influential. Frantz Fanon said in *Black Skins, White Masks* (1952) 'to speak a language is to assume a world, a culture'.[8] He refers to the process by which values and meanings embodied in the language of the colonisers are also adopted by the colonised. This, in turn, affects the mental framework the latter construct to understand their own past.

Consider a not uncommon scenario. A white, middle-class, British male uses the words 'the African experience of decolonisation' while giving a lecture in a college in London. Words are representations of ideas; their function is to produce mental pictures in our minds (meanings). But the words do not have exactly the same meaning for a poor, black, African, female student who has recently arrived in the country to take his course. His 'meaning' might be taken from things he has read in books; hers from experiences she has just left behind. But she will have to read those same books, eventually, and they are only available in English. In other words, to pass her exams she will have to adopt the 'meanings' of decolonisation employed by the kinds of people who write the books and teach the courses. And we all know who they are! If her discourse survives this 'intellectual colonisation', she might question why lectures on decolonisation in the college are never given by black or Asian people. The point is the cultural contexts of the two people are different, power is not equal and this affects which discourse becomes dominant.

To return to Ferro, he is saying that however much a European tries, he or she cannot interpret decolonisation in the same way as the decolonised because the cultural context from which each comes is different. It may even be that what the European regards as an historical account that bends over backwards to be fair will be interpreted by the African or Asian as a way of relieving responsibility, or even guilt.

You might be thinking that we have strayed a long way from history, into philosophy or linguistics perhaps. But I make no apologies for this. The historian, today, has to adopt an inter-disciplinary approach. The ideas one uses are frequently shared with others who interpret human behaviour. In the case we have just been discussing, discourse theory has challenged decolonisation history to refresh itself with new approaches. This can only be enlightening. When the first studies of decolonisation were coming out in the 1960s it was treated as a completed process: definitely history to be put on the shelf. Now we recognise that there are strong continuities passing into the present, and colonialism has assumed new guises. The dragons that nationalists thought they had slain have returned to haunt them as cultural ghosts. Once the enemy was visible as the soldier in a battlefield; now it assumes the insidious disguise of the teacher in the classroom. To combat it, the work of decolonised intellectuals, such as Fanon and Edward Said,[9] has become very important in post-colonial studies.

3 Key Questions in the History of Decolonisation

> **KEY ISSUE** What are some of the more challenging questions that historians focus upon?

Examiners of any topic in modern history will concern themselves with just a few fundamental questions. Do not be deceived by the fact that they seem to find an infinite number of different ways of asking them! These questions need to be raised now because they will inform the argument in the chapters to follow.

a) Why did decolonisation accelerate so rapidly after 1945?

As war broke out in 1939 only a clairvoyant might have predicted that decolonisation would have followed it so swiftly. Yet most decolonisation was over within two decades of 1945. Many developments were unexpected, yet proceeded with breathtaking speed. Why did the European empires come to an end so quickly after the end of the Second World War? What was the connection between war and colonial change?

b) Why were some European powers more prepared to decolonise than others?

More than a decade after the British had left India the French were still immersed in a bitter struggle to avoid leaving Algeria. For more than a decade after the French were forced to leave Algeria, the Portuguese were fighting tooth and nail to cling onto their African Empire. There was clearly a fundamental difference in the propensity to decolonise. Some appeared to leave voluntarily; others reluctantly. The reasons for this are complex. They lie in the different balance of forces present in each empire between metropole and nationalism, and in the strategic implications of each decolonisation for international relations.

c) Why were some decolonisations more violent than others?

Reluctance to decolonise usually made the process more violent and post-colonial instability more likely. But violence often erupted within the decolonised themselves. Ethnic and religious conflicts preceded colonialism, but colonialism's frequent resort to divide and rule tactics made them worse. Some of these antagonisms continued through decolonisation. Finally, the intervention of the superpowers could prolong decolonisation and make it more violent. These factors complicate the process and make it more difficult for the historian to unravel.

d) What economic considerations were at stake over decolonisation?

Bernard Waites has used two useful terms. He has written about the colonial powers drawing up 'a balance sheet of modern colonialism' and doing 'the economic calculus in the decolonisation process'.[10] The issue he points us towards is whether decolonisation took place because colonialism had ceased to be profitable. Perhaps it never had been, or perhaps a new calculus was done that thought that 'neo-colonialism' would be more profitable. These are difficult questions and they produce different balance sheets for different empires. What is not in doubt is that all the decolonising powers placed a high premium upon maintaining good economic relations with their former colonies.

e) How did the Cold War affect decolonisation?

Decolonisation took place within a changing global politics. Between 1945 and 1991 world politics was dominated by the rivalries and conflicts of the two superpowers, the USA and the USSR. Neither was prepared to lose newly independent states to the other's system without a struggle. The Cold War period is, therefore, littered with examples of conflicts in the decolonising world behind which lay the driving forces of American capitalism and Soviet communism. Until the end of the 1950s the USA had the upper hand in this struggle, but in the 1960s the USSR emerged stronger, more determined, and was joined by its ideological ally, Cuba. In the late nineteenth century, the British imperialist Cecil Rhodes had threatened to paint the map of Africa red from the Cape to Cairo. By the 1970s, many in the West thought it had become the ambition of President Leonid Brezhnev of the USSR.

4 Origins of Decolonisation

> **KEY ISSUE** What were the roots of decolonisation within the long-term history of European imperialism?

European colonisation of the non-European world dates from the fifteenth century. From that time onwards improved skills such as those of geometry and shipbuilding enabled first the Portuguese, then others, to sail around the world. Gunpowder became a key technology in imposing their rule upon the 'discovered' peoples. Trade in valuable commodities like gold and spices was immensely profitable. Until the nineteenth century, Asia and the Americas had been the focus of colonisation; Africa had supplied slave labour.

Historians make the distinction between new and old imperialism, that is between colonies acquired during the scramble of the late nineteenth century and those taken before. The scramble for Africa colonised almost the complete continent within a few decades. By 1900 only Abyssinia (later Ethiopia) and Liberia remained independent of European rule. The causes of this rush to colonise are complex, but can be broken down into three.

a) Economic

The European economy had gone into cyclical depression from the early 1870s and further colonisation was thought to be a way of obtaining new markets by which to rescue it. Such hopes proved largely ill founded because Africans had little consuming power, and in the long run their economies were more valuable for providing raw materials than markets. However, the balance sheet of imperialism's worth took a long time to draw up, indeed some historians are still doing it, and some analysts got it wrong at the time. One of these was

Lenin, who thought that imperialism would be capitalism's final stage before it collapsed.

b) Strategic

Problems with the economic explanation of imperialism have led sceptics to offer a strategic alternative to it. This concentrates upon the growing international rivalry of the late nineteenth century, which it must be conceded was partly economic. This led to a rush to colonise places of strategic advantage. Britain in Egypt is often quoted as a good example as it provided a naval vantage point in the Mediterranean, as well as a gateway to India through the Suez Canal.

c) Cultural

Religious reasons figure prominently within this explanation. Missionary zeal in spreading Christianity to the 'dark continents' has to be taken account of. In themselves, these are insufficient to explain the full force of imperialism, but formal colonisation did open up more opportunity for those who wished to spread Christianity.

In conclusion, imperialism had been a way of arranging the world that met the interests of the great powers in the late nineteenth-century. By the second half of the twentieth century, however, the new world powers preferred other arrangements.

5 Decolonisation: a General Outline

> **KEY ISSUES** Identify the principal areas of the world that were decolonised, the decolonising powers and the timescale over which it occurred.

The first half of the twentieth century witnessed the first two world wars in history. It is difficult to exaggerate the impact of these events. Wars of that magnitude and duration drained the resources of colonial nations on an unprecedented scale. Victors as well as vanquished paid an enormous price. The cost for colonialism was political as well as economic. Indian nationalists were the first to present the bill after 1945, and India became the first, and perhaps greatest, of the decolonisations. Largely predictable from developments during the Second World War and before, it nevertheless made a huge impact upon the mentality of Empire. British decolonisation thereafter took on a look of inevitability, although it was not until after the Suez crisis (1956) and Macmillan's 'Wind of Change' speech (1960) that this was officially acknowledged. Before then counter-insurgency wars, as they were called, were fought in Kenya, Malaya and Cyprus against 'guerrilla leaders', some of whom subsequently became the leaders of their countries. Even the country that started the process, Britain, was unable to decolonise completely peacefully. Rhodesia remained an illegal sore point until 1980 but was spared the military intervention witnessed elsewhere. Only Hong Kong was left of any significance after that. It was returned to China in 1997.

It might seem surprising that neither the French, Dutch, Belgians, nor Portuguese rushed to follow the British example in India after 1947. The Dutch recolonised Indonesia after the Japanese left in 1945 and fought to remain. The Belgians showed every intention of remaining in the Congo until a sudden explosion of violence in 1959 caused them to make an about-turn. The French response was more ambivalent. A willingness to vacate sub-Saharan Africa contrasted with the fighting of two colonial wars to remain in Indo-China and Algeria. Both were unsuccessful, and French decolonisation was effectively over by 1962. The Portuguese remained like a dinosaur of colonialism until the mid-1970s. It was a special case, a dictatorship with an archaic colonial ideology, whose decolonisation required the unique response of revolution at home. These examples illustrate that opposition to decolonisation was often very strong, showing that some colonial powers saw empires as more permanent than others. Certainly, decolonisation was not seen as inevitable.

6 Planning Ahead

> **KEY ISSUE** How can each chapter help answer the key questions about decolonisation?

So far, this introduction might have pointed towards the history of decolonisation being an enormously complex one. It is problematic in that there is disagreement amongst historians over how to use the term, the timescale of the process, its causes and, not least, how to broadly evaluate its effects. This uncertainty leads to the use by historians of theories or models for the purpose of interpreting what is contentious. No single model is likely to be complete – theories by their very nature never are – and we are likely to have to pick and choose between them, selecting what we regard as the most useful ideas.

At this point, it is necessary to be more optimistic and confident about the task ahead. We have set ourselves a number of clearly framed key questions which can be answered to the satisfaction of examiners. A selective approach has been adopted which is manageable, namely a limited investigation of the decolonisations by the five main colonial powers. This should enable us to apply a genuinely comparative approach and to reach a conclusion as to whether there is an historical process to be recognised, rather than just a set of largely different experiences.

Chapter 2 examines the origins of decolonisation between the end of the First World War and the start of the Second. It is primarily concerned to show how war and economic depression weakened empires and laid the pre-conditions for decolonisation. Chapter 3 principally examines British decolonisation in India, Malaya, the Middle East and Africa in the context of its decline as a world power. Chapter 4 asks why French decolonisation in Indo-China and Algeria resulted in colonial wars when a more peaceful pattern typified sub-Saharan Africa. Chapter 5 is an exercise in comparative history. From a study of Dutch, Belgian and Portuguese decolonisations, it asks whether any general patterns can be detected when compared with the British and French cases. Finally, Chapter 6 returns to the causes, key questions, and consequences of decolonisation and offers some summarised answers.

Summary Diagram
Origins of decolonisation

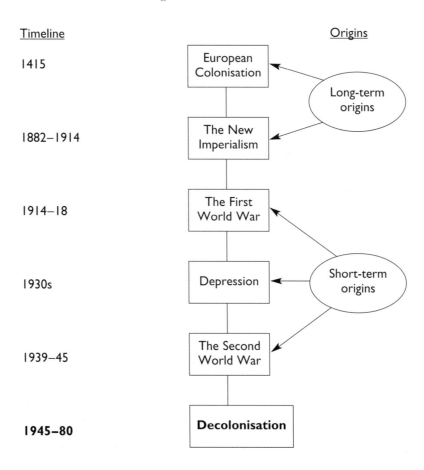

Timeline		Origins
1415	European Colonisation	Long-term origins
1882–1914	The New Imperialism	
1914–18	The First World War	
1930s	Depression	Short-term origins
1939–45	The Second World War	
1945–80	**Decolonisation**	

References

1 Marc Ferro, *Colonization: a global history* (Routledge, 1997).
2 Raymond Betts, *Decolonization* (Routledge, 1998).
3 Quoted in Anthony Kirk-Greene, 'Decolonisation in British Africa', *History Today*, January 1992, p.50.
4 T.E. Vadney, *The World Since 1945* (Penguin, 1998), p.88
5 Paul Kennedy, *The Rise and Fall of the Great Powers: Economic Change and Military Conflict from 1500 to 2000* (Fontana, 1989).
6 Kennedy, *The Rise and Fall*, p.505.
7 Ferro, *Colonization*, p.vii.
8 Quoted in Betts, *Decolonization*, p.86.
9 Edward Said, *Culture and Imperialism* (Chatto and Windus, 1993).
10 Bernard Waites, *Europe and the Third World: from Colonialism to Decolonisation, c.1500–1998* (Macmillan, 1999), chapters 7 and 8.

2 War, Depression and Empires 1919–39

POINTS TO CONSIDER

This chapter examines the long-term causes of decolonisation. Although the Second World War had the most decisive effect in ending the European empires, both the First World War and the events of the inter-war period, notably economic depression, also played an important role. It focuses upon the way in which the First World War led to a new environment of international relations and how European imperialism had to be restructured to take account of it. Finally, it demonstrates how economic depression placed strains upon political relationships within the empires, making them vulnerable to the assault of the Second World War.

KEY DATES

1918 End of First World War
1919 Treaty of Versailles; Amritsar massacre in India
1926 Indonesian Insurrection
1927 National Party of Vietnam founded
1929 Wall Street Crash
1932 Ottawa Conference
1935 Government of India Act
1937 Formation of Algerian Popular Party
1939 Outbreak of the Second World War

1 The Effects of the First World War

KEY ISSUES How did the First World War end the empires of the defeated powers and to what extent did the mandate system strengthen those of the victors?

In February 1918, the Allies agreed a blueprint for the new international order once the war had ended. It became known as 'The 14 Points.' The American President, Woodrow Wilson, took a leading role in this. He was critical of European imperialism and the fifth point recommended:

1   a free, open-minded and absolutely impartial adjustment of all colonial
    claims, based upon a strict observance of the principle that in deter-
    mining all such questions of sovereignty the interests of the populations
    concerned must have equal weight with the equitable claims of the gov-
5   ernment whose title is to be determined.[1]

This is often taken to be a general statement about how all colonies should be treated. In theory, this is how it was intended; in practice, Wilson was thinking mainly of the empires of the defeated powers Germany, Austria-Hungary and Turkey, which he did not want to be swallowed up by the existing empires of the Allies. In order to prevent this, he had to concede that Britain and France were not going to give up their empires. The Mandate System was established by which the victors became responsible for the defeated powers' former colonies, without their actually being absorbed into those victor powers' empires.

In Germany's former colonies the new obligations extended only to supplying 'good and humane government'. This was to be provided by the British in Tanganyika (formerly German E. Africa), by South Africa in the former German S.W. Africa, Australia in New Guinea and other Pacific islands, New Zealand in W. Samoa. Togoland and the Cameroons were divided between British and French authority.

In the former Turkish territories, however, Britain and France were given the responsibility of bringing their mandates to independence as soon as possible. But the British in Palestine and Transjordan, and the French in Syria and the Lebanon, behaved as if they had been given additions to empire. Only the British mandate of Iraq achieved independence before the Second World War (in 1932). No peoples of the mandated territories were consulted as to their wishes. Conservatives like Arthur Balfour only ever saw it as an experimental system. Liberals tended to agree with the historian H.A.L. Fisher, that the notion of trusteeship in the mandates 'draped the crudity of conquest in a veil of morality'.

The Permanent Mandates Commission set up by the new League of Nations challenged the assumption that empires were to continue unchanged. A key task was to take account of the wishes of their peoples in moving the territories towards 'self-determination'. The problem was that because most members of the Permanent Commission came from colonial powers they showed little interest in 'self-determination'. The phrase was, in any case, vague and open to interpretation. The League did little to admonish members who ignored its instructions.

The British and the French mandates ran into difficulties by the 1930s. In Iraq, the British steadily devolved power after an insurrection in 1920. By 1932, they were content to save the expense of direct rule and cede independence in return for the retention of military bases and access to oil supplies. In Palestine, the Arabs already distrusted the British due to the support of the Balfour Declaration (1917) for the principle of a Jewish homeland (see page 47). Allowing more Jewish immigration through the 1930s added to distrust. Transjordan was less of a problem. A weak buffer state between Saudi Arabia and Palestine, it was heavily dependent upon British aid and investment. French behaviour in their mandates made the British appear a model of restraint. In the Lebanon, French neglect provoked a revolt in 1925. In Syria, the record was little different, and although, in 1936, the French promised both the Lebanese and the Syrians progress towards self-government within three years, they had still not carried this out by 1939.

2 Constraints upon Imperial Confidence

> **KEY ISSUE** Why did developments in the inter-war period make the administration of empires more difficult?

Eric Hobsbawm has pointed to the paradox that the British, in the inter-war period, found themselves ruling over more territory than ever with less confidence. That reduced confidence can be applied to all the imperialist powers and was rooted in several factors, which Robert Holland has termed 'stiffening constraints'.[2]

a) Demographic changes

The first of these was demographic (related to population). Populations were rising fast and colonial agriculture had to provide more food if stable rule was to be maintained. This conflicted with the established practice of taking over the local peasant economy and running it for the benefit of the colonisers and their collaborators amongst the local landlords. In French Indo-China, for example, rice and rubber were exported while the landless poor roamed the countryside in search of work. They often turned to the growing nationalist and communist movements.

b) Changes in class structure: an emerging colonial middle class

The new colonial middle class led such movements, and they are the second constraint. The formation of an urban middle class in the colonies was caused by the initial stages of industrialisation. Administering colonies required large bureaucracies sited in regional centres of trade and commerce. These indigenous middle classes began to agitate politically. Indian nationalism illustrates how this process developed first in the Asian colonies. Leaders such as Jawaharlal Nehru and Mohandas Gandhi were lawyers. Behind them was a developing entrepreneurial class who had done well out of the First World War and saw the Congress Party as the means of further progress.

c) Religion

Many historians have recognised the connection between religion and economic depression. E.P. Thompson once described the tendency of the eighteenth-century English poor to seek escape through millenarianism (belief in the imminent Second Coming of Christ as Saviour) as 'the chiliasm of despair'. A chiliast is one who believes that the millennium is nigh. Christian millenarianism emerged in Nyasaland, Central Africa. But religious revivalism extended beyond this. Hinduism (in India), Islam (in Indonesia) and Buddhism (in Burma) also articulated the differences between the colonised and their colonisers. Religious revivalism was not merely a reaction to poverty caused by depression, but also a rejection of Western belief-systems that were blamed for their suffering by colonised peoples. Islamic fundamentalism has played an analogous role in more recent times.

3 Nationalism

> **KEY ISSUE** The rise of nationalism was one of the causes of decolonisation after 1945. But how developed was it in the inter-war period?

a) The nature of nationalism

Historians used to see nationalism as a great unifier of peoples in the modern world. A 'deep down nationalism' was supposed to have united Italians, Germans and others in nineteenth-century Europe. Few believe in this any longer. In its place, historians see people making choices based upon economic self-interest. This revisionism has spread into the history of decolonisation. We should not exaggerate the similarities between nineteenth-century Europe and twentieth-century Asia and Africa. But there are some. Empires ended and new nation states were created in their wake. But one of the great errors of decolonisation was to create new nations by using the old imperialist frontiers that had never been drawn to include 'nations' of people. Hence, the new states contained peoples with many fundamental differences. In the circumstances, it is hardly surprising that decolonisation has not always brought national cohesion. Sometimes it has brought its opposite, and there are several African examples where the state has completely broken down after decolonisation.

These considerations should lead us to treat nationalism cautiously. It has been presented as an heroic Jack slaying the dastardly Giant of imperialism. There is much evidence for this positive view. It did confront racist ideas such as that Asians and Africans could not make best use of their own resources and needed leadership by Europeans. But sometimes nationalism was really no more than anti-colonialism. It united people temporarily against a common enemy. Once that enemy was expelled, it dissolved into numerous smaller identities, ethnic, tribal or religious.

b) Nationalism in Asia and Africa

In the early twentieth century, Japan was a model for the Asian nationalist. Its ability to resist imperialism was widely admired, but, paradoxically, so too were its imperialist achievements, such as the defeat of Russia in the war of 1904–5. Japan's influence was strongest in neighbouring territories such as French Indo-China, as the following statement by a young nationalist shows:

1   Having had the opportunity to study new books and new doctrines, I, an obscure student that I was, discovered in a recent history of Japan how she was able to conquer the impotent Europeans. It is for this reason that we have formed an organization ... We have the most
5   energetic and courageous of young Annamese [a region of Indo-China] to send them for study to Japan. Several years elapsed without the French being aware of this movement ...To prepare the people for the future is but our sole aim.[3]

As well as illustrating the power of history, this document gives a strong sense of a new civilisation being built in Asia. Far from following European models, the author writes that continent off as 'impotent'. The French were too stupid to realise that Annamese nationalists were going to be educated and trained in Tokyo! The future lay with them, not with moribund imperialists. The document shows the cross-fertilisation of Asian nationalism in this period. The Chinese nationalists, the Kuomintang, were also admired as stalwarts of the anti-imperialist movement, until the Communists eclipsed them in the late 1940s. For all the condescension shown here towards the imperialists, Asian nationalists fed from the hand they bit. They took on board European ideas of government and technological development, and built careers in the bureaucracy. Lawyers scuttled through every corridor, searching for a job to match their qualifications. Under-employed ones turned their hands to politics.

We have already noted the religious revival of the inter-war period that was turned against imperialism. Islam had been undergoing a revival since before the First World War under the intellectual guidance of Cairo. The war, however, fractured Muslim unity as some territories like Egypt fought with Britain and her allies; others like Turkey on the side of the Central Powers. At the end of the war, Islamic nationalism was strongest amongst the Arabs, notably in Egypt, which soon freed itself from British rule (1922). By 1931 some measure of unity was restored at the World Islamic Conference where the agenda consisted of the defence of all Islamic peoples against imperialism.

The reason for African nationalism evolving more slowly than Asian is commonly given as Africa's relative under-development. But only the interior was under-developed. Many of the coastal areas had been highly developed through trade. A good example was the East coast, where the great Swahili civilisation had been built upon commercial links with Asia. Neither could the North be described as under-developed. Cairo was an intellectual centre of the Muslim world, led by the great Islamic moderniser Professor Jamal al-Din al Afghani.

African nationalism also owed something in its origins to the Italian invasion of Ethiopia in 1935. Italy had made a previous attack upon Ethiopia in 1896, from its existing colony in Eritrea. It was repelled at the Battle of Adowa in a triumph that entered the folklore of African history. When a fascist government under Mussolini took power in Italy, intent upon national regeneration through imperialist war, it sought revenge. Despite a personal appeal by the Emperor Halie Selassie to the League of Nations in Geneva it offered no intervention, only verbal condemnation. The young Kwame Nkrumah, later prime minister of Ghana, was a student in London at the time and describes in his autobiography how these events intensified his nationalism and steeled his determination to end colonialism. Out of these events 'Ethiopianism' was born, and this sympathy with the colonisation of a great and proud African people was to give birth to the Rastafarianism of our own times. When its latter-day prophet, Bob Marley, urged an exodus, 'a movement of Ja people' back to Ethiopia in the 1960s, he was following in the footsteps of his fellow Jamaican Marcus Garvey, who had urged Afro-Caribbeans to go 'back to Africa' in the inter-war period. Unlike Garvey, Marley preserved the historical memory through the traditional African medium of song.

Finally, we must turn to the influence of socialism upon nationalism. Historians like Grimal, writing in the 1960s at a time when the Soviet Union was a superpower, probably exaggerated the influence of Marxism. Lenin himself in his *Thesis on national and colonial questions* (1920) recognised its weakness in the less developed countries, where the proletariat was small or non-existent. The peasantry were dispersed and politically unorganised. Neither class, on its own, was likely to lead an anti-imperialist movement, let alone a socialist one. In contrast, Lenin observed the bourgeoisie organising politically at a faster rate. They were likely to be the leaders of the anti-imperialist struggle. Therefore, he urged communists to attach themselves to the broad, nationalist movement, expel the imperialists, and worry about making socialism afterwards.

When Ho Chi Minh adopted this strategy in Indo-China he was successful in building a strong, nationalist movement. But when the Indonesian Communists (PKI) relied solely upon the peasantry during the insurrection of 1926 they failed, for which they were bitterly criticised by Stalin:

The PKI, despite considerable effort, has not succeeded in its campaign to persuade the peasants to join the nationalist movement. The mistakes the Indonesian comrades made in their relations with the nationalist organizations were repeated in their dealings with the peasantry.[4]

Socialism was essentially a European doctrine. It was developed by thinkers like Karl Marx in response to historical conditions that evolved in Europe, namely industrialisation and the formation of class society. Colonial societies in Asia and Africa were not like this, so when they imported socialism they had difficulty adapting it to their different circumstances.

4 The Effects of Economic Depression

> **KEY ISSUE** How serious was the depression in the colonies and in what ways did it weaken empires?

a) Falling prices

The inter-war depression strained colonial relations. For the colonies depression began long before the Wall Street Crash of 1929, with the fall in agricultural prices from the early 1920s. This made it more difficult for colonial economies to trade with industrial ones because they were receiving lower prices for their exports of primary goods. Economic historians call this a deterioration in the 'terms of trade' of the colonial economies. When permitted, colonies looked beyond the imperial relationship in order to survive. For example, the Indian economy by turning towards other sources of investment became less important to Britain. On the other hand, the Portuguese colonial economies were entirely ring-fenced.

b) Discontent and protest

Another effect of depression and falling prices was a wave of strikes that swept across the colonial economies. Amongst the most serious were those that affected the Central African copper belt between 1935 and 1940. This region, which overlapped the British territory of Northern Rhodesia and the region of the Belgian Congo called Katanga, had already seen a great deal of social dislocation caused by rural-urban migration. On the other side of the world, strikes also broke out in the British Caribbean islands of Trinidad and Jamaica. Although Trinidad had developed oil and asphalt industries and Jamaica bauxite, the historians of the West Indies write:

> The price of sugar was still the barometer of West Indian prosperity... but it began to fall in 1923, and fell catastrophically after 1929 to reach the lowest figure in its history – less than £5 per ton – in 1934 ... a fact

to be borne in mind when discussing the riots and disturbances of
5 1935–38.⁵

The fact that the price of the staple crop, sugar, had not merely fallen
a lot, but had reached an all-time low is a stark indicator of the seri-
ousness of depression on the colonial economies. Eric Hobsbawm has
argued that this led to a mass political mobilisation, questioning the
very nature of the colonial relationship, especially in the cash crop
economies of West Africa and South East Asia.⁶ In French Indo-
China, and in North Africa, the first serious challenges to colonial
rule began to be made. In India, the nationalist movement that had
existed since before the First World War made its first real links with
the masses through the non-cooperation movement. But except in
India, the upsurge of militancy did not indicate that mass movements
were close to overthrowing colonialism. The depression weakened
empires but did not lead to their breakdown.

5 The British Empire between the Wars

> **KEY ISSUE** What were the most significant changes in the British
> Empire during this period?

a) The economic consequences of war and depression

The disruption of international trade caused by the First World War
caused Britain to lose many important export markets outside the
empire. This led to imperial markets assuming a greater importance
within the nation's balance of payments. But trade with the empire
had also declined as a result of war; it had just declined less. The inter-
war years, however, saw a recovery of trade with the empire, particularly the white dominions. The exception was India, which moved
from being a debtor to a creditor economy in its relations with
Britain.

Until 1932 Britain was a free trading economy. As depression took
hold, however, it was forced to introduce protection outside of the
empire although not within it. At the Ottawa Conference of 1932
Britain wanted free trade with the Dominions and India but they
insisted on keeping some tariffs. Instead the system of imperial preference was adopted. Each side charged lower tariffs and guaranteed
quotas of trade to the other. These conditions helped the Dominions
but worsened Britain's balance of payments. The Dominions actually
exported more in value to Britain after 1932 than before, while
Britain's exports to them fell. With India and the other crown
colonies, there was a similar pattern. Exports to Britain fell but by a
smaller margin than imports from Britain. Thus, Cain and Hopkins
have argued, it was the manufacturing exporters who paid the price

of depression. The 'gentlemanly capitalists,' that is the bankers of the City of London, succeeded in maintaining the dominance of British finance capital within the empire.

b) India

At the end of the First World War, India had a considerable debt to Britain. Thus, British policy in India in the inter-war period sought to create a budget surplus by which she could pay Britain back. This was eventually achieved, for example through the protection of the Indian textile industry that allowed it to grow at the expense of Lancashire's. There were still some economic difficulties in the inter-war period. The rupee was over-valued in relation to the pound and this affected Indian exports by making them more expensive. The political campaign to boycott British goods in 1931 also affected exports. Finally, the banking system had to be improved to attract capital investment with confidence.

Both war and depression fuelled the rise of nationalism in India. One and a half million Indians had fought in the war and far more paid increased taxes. But nationalists felt Britain lacked gratitude. They wanted self-governing status like the dominions. When the 1919 Government of India Act only offered provincial autonomy over such things as education and health, and a central parliament with very limited responsibility, mass protest broke out. The more radical leaders of the Congress Party (founded in 1906), like M.K. Gandhi, called a general strike. In March 1919, the Rowlatt Act allowed for imprisonment of 'extremists' without trial for up to two years. At Amritsar in April, an unarmed crowd of some 5,000 gathered illegally to protest against the Act. A British force commanded by General Reginald Dyer was ordered to shoot into it, killing 379.

Gandhi was appalled at the massacre. He urged the politics of peaceful, non-cooperation or *satyagraha*, but when it turned to violence he was arrested. Pleading guilty in 1922 to inciting disaffection to the government, he was sentenced to six years' imprisonment but was released after two. Through the 1920s periods of ungovernability became common. By the end of the decade, leaders such as Gandhi and Nehru, from an educated, urban middle class the like of which were still to emerge in colonial Africa, found that considerable powers of disruption lay in their hands. Gandhi was more moderate than Nehru in his demands, for when Nehru demanded immediate independence in 1928, Gandhi spoke only for dominion status within a year. When neither was forthcoming, mass civil disobedience campaigns followed, ranging from refusals to pay taxation to strikes by schoolchildren, desertions from the army, and the boycotting of British goods. Arresting Gandhi and Nehru and suspending the Congress Party could not disguise the fact that only a change of policy by the British was likely to end the protests.

Since the end of the war the British had been extending representative government in India and by 1930 the Simon Report recommended progress towards Dominion status. This led to the
London Conference on India's constitutional status, but it was
unlikely to be successful when the leading Indian figures were kept in
prison. By the time he was released in 1931 Gandhi had moved much
closer to Nehru over the need for immediate independence. Instead,
the British passed the Government of India Act (1935). It granted
provincial self-government but this still left the Viceroy in control of
important matters such as foreign policy. Congress opposed it as a
measure to contain its power, which it thought would be greater in a
unitary state. But it did contest elections under the new constitution
and the fact that it won majorities in most provincial assemblies gave
it the capacity to make representative government unworkable. This
it did when the Viceroy declared war in 1939 without consulting
Indian legislatures.

c) British Africa

In Africa, the British imperial hold looked much more secure than in
India. A main reason for this was the relative under-development of
the colonies, which held back nationalism of the strength found in
India. Africa never amounted to more than 3 per cent of the British
export market in the inter-war period. It tended to be a refuge for
uncompetitive manufacturers. The smart money of the 'gentlemanly
capitalists' of the City went elsewhere. Under-investment undermined
the intention of making the African economies self-sufficient. The
colonial administrations tried to substitute their own investment for
the lack of private capital, but they could not raise enough taxation
from the local populations for investment. They were forced to look
for foreign investment, but lacked the revenue to pay back loans.
Through the 1920s colonial development was held back by the economic conservatism of the Treasury refusing to make loans interest
free.

Economic under-development was not the only reason for Africa's
slower progress towards decolonisation. Colonial frontiers in Africa
were no respecters of tribal divisions. Most territories contained a
number of different tribes, and tribes were divided between territories. This made it more difficult to achieve the degree of solidarity
between peoples necessary for an effective anti-colonialist movement.
Social hierarchies were exploited by the British through the system of
indirect rule, widely employed in West Africa and in Uganda.
Pioneered by Lord Lugard in Nigeria between 1912 and 1918, it
involved the Governor or High Commissioner of a territory delegat-
ing to local chiefs everyday functions of government, such as tax collection. This made the local chiefs stakeholders in the colonial
system, and their new authority needed to be bolstered by what

Terence Ranger has called 'the invention of tradition'.[7] This involved the creation of rituals and ceremonies to celebrate the spurious longevity of a chief's dynasty. Sir James Currie, one-time Director of Education in the Sudan, dismissed this searching for 'lost tribes and vanished chiefs' as illusory. Benedict Anderson has written about the way in which the culture of nationalist movements creates 'imagined communities' in the past, to provide their supporters with a sense of identity and justification.[8] What both these views remind us is that history is a series of competing narratives, constantly being rewritten, sometimes to suit the agendas of politicians. Urban nationalists tended to see through this, which was what the Governors of the Sudan feared when they declared in 1920 that their purpose was to 'strengthen the solid elements in the countryside ... before the irresponsible body of half-educated officials, students and town riff-raff takes control of the public mind'.[9]

If indirect rule had any saving grace it was that it did maintain ownership of the land by Africans, even if only by a few Africans. Yet, in Holland's opinion it was '... a blunt and inefficient instrument'[10] as a system of colonial government. Prospects of any kind of national self-government remained in the distant future. Opinions like those of Lord Lugard reflected the British interpretation of its trusteeship. 'We hold these countries because it is the genius of our race to colonise, to trade and to govern.'[11] Such statements revealed not so much that Lugard had been born in India, but that he had been educated at Sandhurst and remained a devout Christian with a sense of mission. Trusteeship had been conferred upon Britain after the First World War. Men like Lugard welcomed it as an opportunity to redefine the imperial mission, not to abandon it. Pioneered in Kenya from 1923 trusteeship centralised control in the hands of the Governor, and had the advantage of keeping it out of the hands of the white settlers. Any kind of power delegated to black Africans was unthinkable to them. The situation was different in West Africa where there were few white settlers.

The Union of South Africa, created in 1910, was a strong influence upon the white populations of the British East and Central African colonies. Although it did not adopt the policies that became known as apartheid until after the Second World War, it did discriminate between the wars, by denying non-whites the vote in parliamentary elections after 1936. Moreover, as a fast-developing economy, whites elsewhere in Africa looked upon South Africa as a model. This was the case in the Crown Colony of Southern Rhodesia, although white Rhodesians showed no desire for political incorporation into South Africa. Granted self-government in 1923 as a viable economic unit, Southern Rhodesia had more to lose than gain by amalgamation.

The depression of the 1930s caught the African colonies in a vice. The fall in export prices reduced taxation revenue to the administrations. This, in turn, made it impossible to pay back foreign loans.

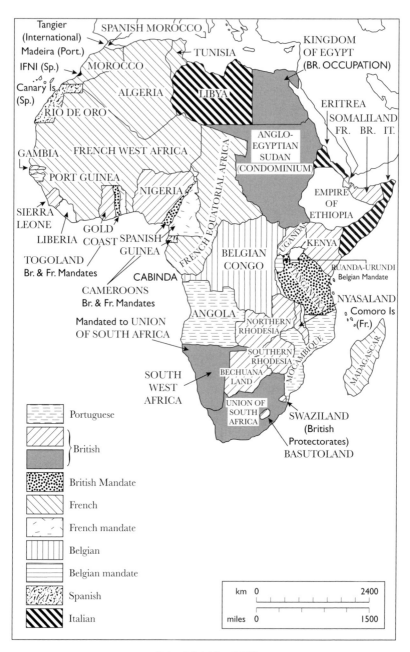

Colonial Africa 1925

London, however, still insisted upon balanced budgets, so public expenditure was reduced and tax collection made more efficient. Both added to African complaints about colonial rule. Small measures in the 1930s designed to improve land management and productivity did little to satisfy them. War broke upon British Africa in 1939 after two decades of under-investment and neglect.

6 The French Empire between the Wars

> **KEY ISSUE** How much did French imperialism change during this period, both in theory and practice?

a) Changes in the practice of French imperialism

A key concept of French imperialism, known as 'assimilation', perceived colonies as one and indivisible from France. In the official mind, France had no colonies, only departments. In the case of the older departments like Algeria, they had direct political representation in Paris. Algerian deputies could sit alongside those from any other department, like Normandy or Provence. Children in colonial classrooms looked up to the command 'Children, love France, your new fatherland'. One sceptical Frenchman observed that assimilation assumed ' ... that what makes us happy will make everyone happy, that all of humanity must feel and think as France does.'[12]

Behind this façade of what Betts calls 'cultural condescension' lay a racial reality. The majority of colonies were not given representation in the French Parliament because that would have produced a non-white majority there. So the official mind emphasised 'equalities', such as equality before the law, as being important. Nevertheless, while Algerians took seats in Paris, no Indian sat at Westminster. Most French colonial subjects, however, had to make do with purely advisory local assemblies, on which they were a minority. The worst colonies still used forced labour, as the Portuguese did. No free trade unions were allowed until 1937. Despite what they said, the French never regarded the empire as vitally important. Investment was neglected and only the least competitive business interests took refuge there.

The effect of the First World War and the Mandate system was to change the language, if not the reality, of French imperialism. The new ideology pronounced that the colonies were to be developed for the benefit of the whole world. The League of Nations passed on that duty of trust to the international community, and to Mandated members in particular. In practice, however, there was minimal supervision of such obligations, and the French were able to carry on imperialist business as usual. Nevertheless, a change in *mentalité* did occur in France and can be detected in literature. White writers wrote less about the need for expansion and more about humanism and leadership; the Martiniquan Paul Maran became the first black writer to win the celebrated Goncourt prize in 1921, with his novel *Batouala*, examining colonialism from the experience of the colonised. Such thinking was to be found notably on the Left where the Socialist Party urged preparing the colonies for self-government at the earliest opportunity. However, when they were given the opportunity, in the Popular Front Government between 1935 and 1938, opposition to their plans overwhelmed the Socialists.

b) North Africa

Despite the fine words of the Minister for the Colonies, 'A colonial system cannot survive unless it is operated from within by the natives who are supposed to benefit from it',[13] the Algerian *pieds noirs* (white settlers of French origins) blocked all attempts at reform. All the government could manage was the enfranchisement of a few thousand more Algerians in 1937. Most Muslims preferred to remain voteless rather than relinquish Islamic law for French. They had been disappointed in the promise of citizenship after the First World War and expected little from Paris as a result. Marc Ferro has described French rule in Algeria as a dehumanising and racist colonialism. It was institutionalised in the law and in education. He quotes the reply of a French witness to a crime who, asked whether there were any other witnesses, said: 'Yes, five, two men and three Arabs.'[14] Ferro taught in Algeria between the wars. He recalls an occasion when, on telling his French pupils that after the fall of the Roman Empire and the rise of Christianity he would teach them the history of Arab civilisation, they fell about laughing. Algerian parents failed to see the joke. Only 5.4 per cent of Muslim children went to French schools in 1930, largely because of the condescension shown towards Arabic, which was not even a compulsory subject. Arabic schools were strictly limited by licence. Illegal ones were vigorously prosecuted, which reduced the Muslim population to a state of near illiteracy.

By the 1930s, this had driven nationalists to play up cultural differences. As one leader, Ben Badis, put it: 'Islam is our religion, Algeria our country, Arabic our language.'[15] Furthermore, this separatist nationalism extended its reach across the Mediterranean to the working-class, immigrant suburbs of French cities. In 1937 nationalists united in the Algerian Popular Party, which demanded nothing less than complete independence from France. This was some way from the intellectual-led movement of the post-war period, which had accepted 'assimilation' and demanded only better government by the French.

Elsewhere in North Africa, Moroccan and Tunisian grievances were similar to those of Algerians. Moroccans complained about unjust land seizures and the marginalisation of the Sultan in govern-

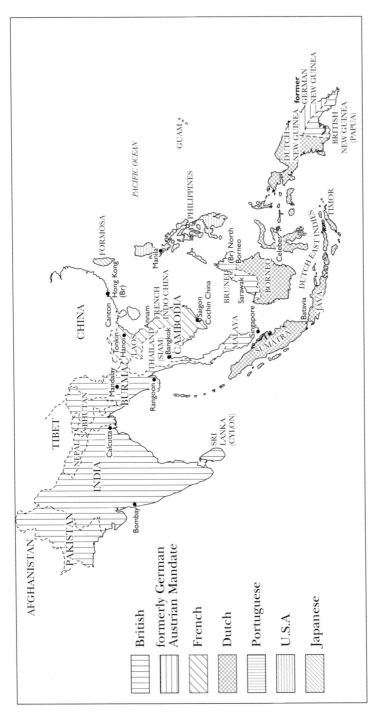

AFGHANISTAN

PAKISTAN

INDIA

TIBET

NEPAL

BHUTAN

Bombay

Calcutta

SRI LANKA (CYLON)

BURMA

Mandalay

Rangoon

CHINA

FORMOSA

Canton

Hong Kong (Br)

Tonkin

Hanoi

LAOS

Annam

THAILAND (SIAM)

Bangkok

FRENCH INDO CHINA

CAMBODIA

Saigon

Cochin China

PACIFIC OCEAN

GUAM

PHILIPPINES

Manila

BRUNEI

Sarawak

North Borneo (Br)

BORNEO

Celebes

DUTCH EAST INDIES

TIMOR

DUTCH NEW GUINEA

former GERMAN NEW GUINEA

BRITISH NEW GUINEA (PAPUA)

MALAYA

Singapore

SUMATRA

Batavia

JAVA

Colonial Asia 1940

British

formerly German Austrian Mandate

French

Dutch

Portuguese

U.S.A

Japanese

ment. A revolt in 1925 had led to the imposition of direct rule from Paris, but a nationalist movement continued to operate from exile. In 1934, the Young Moroccans, royalist followers of Shakib Arslan, decided to press for the Sultan to be restored as head of state, but could not convince the anti-monarchical section of the nationalist movement. In Tunisia, the position of the Bey was similar to that of the Moroccan Sultan. The Young Tunisians supported his claim to the restoration of a constitutional monarchy. From 1927, however, the broader, more modern movement of the lawyer and journalist Habib Bourguiba outflanked them. By 1934 he had built a party, *Neo-Destour* (New Constitution), that spanned both class and religion and demanded independence. Despite its moderate tactics, it was met with repression by the authorities at the behest of the white settler class.

c) Indo-China

The French had first imposed themselves upon the ancient and proud culture of Indo-China in the 1850s. The Indo-Chinese were worked and taxed hard; there had been a tax strike as early as 1907. The First World War ended with French promises of reform to the Indo-Chinese who had fought with them. But, as in North Africa, the white settler class resisted. Therefore, co-operation, turned into opposition, and in 1927 the National Party of Vietnam was founded, determined to end French rule altogether. Its leader was Ho Chi Minh, a communist who thought his homeland was not yet ready for communism. Yet, as communism spread, Asia in the 1930s was fast becoming a political minefield for colonialism. From China to Vietnam the colonialist became identified as an exploiter analogous to the bourgeois exploiter of the European proletariat. French economic policy in Indochina gave credence to this Marxist analysis. The Indo-Chinese economy had been turned into one of cash crops for export. As rice and rubber flowed out of the country, peasants found it increasingly impossible to support a growing population. It is not surprising that in Indo-China the French faced their most serious challenge to empire before the Second World War.

7 The Dutch, Belgian and Portuguese Empires between the Wars

> **KEY ISSUE** How did factors such as war, depression and the rise of nationalism affect these three empires during this period?

The Dutch East Indies between the wars provides another example of the convergence of economic pressures and rising nationalism. As in

India, nationalism began to organise before 1914 and was led by educated members of the middle classes. Dutch neutrality during the First World War meant there had been less instability for it to feed upon. After the Russian Revolution of 1917, however, a Communist Party split from the nationalist movement. It led a failed communist insurrection in 1926. As in China and Vietnam it drew support from a peasantry whose living standards were being assaulted by economic depression. However, Dutch rule was uncompromising, which only served to create greater support for the Japanese when they invaded in 1942.

The Belgian Congo appeared to be amongst the most stable of colonies during the inter-war period, although it did go through significant changes. Despite Belgium's involvement in the First World War, the Congo's central position in Africa left it largely untouched by the military conflict. The inter-war period saw considerable economic development as big mining companies were encouraged by the Belgian government to move in and develop the precious minerals. Because the Congo was industrialising, it survived the depression better than the purely agricultural economies, although it still suffered price falls. However, continued economic development stored up social disruption for the future. The social infrastructure of the towns could not cope with the massive rural-urban migration that took place. Social stability in the Congo became dependent upon the price of copper and diamonds in the world market. Yet, before the 1950s, nationalism in the Congo, as in most of Africa, remained a development for the future.

Portugal had reluctantly joined the First World War on the side of the Allies in 1915 but got precious little out of it. Rather, the cost proved enormously damaging to an already weak economy and its colonialism. As a poor European state, Portugal suffered from chronic under-investment and the colonies were seen as a means of compensating for this. A military coup of 1926 put paid to experiments in opening up the colonial economies, and throughout the 1930s they were completely isolated from world markets, as the Salazar regime sought to spread the meagre rewards of such protection across the small ruling elite it represented. Thus, the Portuguese colonies were as protected from world conditions of depression as it was possible to be. However, this merely guaranteed continued impoverishment, aggravated by the rod of iron that was Portuguese colonial administration under the dictatorship. Poverty and repression combined to hold back nationalism in the inter-war period.

8 Assessment

> **KEY ISSUE** To what extent can we locate the origins of
> decolonisation in the inter-war period?

The First World War was, by definition, the first global war involving peoples from all continents. Yet, the colonised peoples had less stake in what was essentially a conflict over European issues. It is understandable that they expected some reward for participation, especially as they were colonised not free peoples. Those hopes were largely disappointed by the new world order that emanated from the Versailles settlement of 1919. The victorious European powers clung on to the best part of their empires, whatever the fine print of the treaties implied.

But the world had really changed. The war had strengthened the economic position of many colonies within the empires, broadened experience through worldwide participation, expanded horizons through contact with new ideas. By 1919, the colonies were less dependent and more confident than they had been before the war. When the League of Nations consistently failed them, whether over trusteeship or Ethiopia, they were inclined to write it off as a white man's club.

Yet, consciousness of the failings of the restored colonial world order and the capacity to change it are two different things. Power, Mao Zedong once famously observed, comes out of a gun barrel. But being Chinese and a communist he was less inclined to admit that it also comes out of places like the City of London and the French Bourse. International capitalism went through its most serious crisis in modern history during the inter-war period. Colonial economies with their dependence upon primary production were the first and hardest hit. The crash in primary prices through the 1920s reduced living standards in colonial societies where there were no welfare systems to fall back upon.

Such economic circumstances made political organisation for the majority of the colonised impossible. But not all colonial economies were at the same levels of development. In parts of Asia like India and Indo-China quite rapid development had led to nationalism growing before the First World War. After the war, restored imperialism and economic depression both conspired to suffocate it, but the infant refused to expire. It found most oxygen in those colonies whose economic and social modernisation had produced an urban middle class. Yet it must still be stressed that, before 1939, nationalism drew breath in only a few places in Asia and hardly at all in Africa. It was an irritation rather than a threat to empire. No imperialist power imminently contemplated decolonisation before the Second World War. Hence, our assessment must be that imperialism had survived both the war and depression damaged, but not broken. If the Lion no longer roared, it had a few growls left in it. But we should not employ this imperialist imagery uncritically. The Lion was a symbolic appropriation of empire. It belonged naturally to the non-European peoples. And, it was about to be reclaimed by another war and its consequences.

References

1 Henri Grimal, *Decolonization: the British, French, Dutch and Belgian Empires 1919–1963* (Routledge, 1978), p.12.
2 R.F. Holland, *European Decolonisation 1918–81: An Introductory Survey* (Macmillan, 1985), p.2.
3 Grimal, *Decolonization*, p.40.
4 *Ibid.*, p.34.
5 J.H. Parry and Philip Sherlock, *A History of the West Indies* (Macmillan, 1971), pp.285–6.
6 Eric Hobsbawm, *Age of Extremes. The Short Twentieth Century 1914–91* (Abacus, 1994), p.214.
7 E.J. Hobsbawm and T.O. Ranger, eds., *The Invention of Tradition* (Cambridge University Press, 1983).
8 Benedict Anderson, *Imagined Communities: Reflections on the Origin and Spread of Nationalism* (Verso, 1991).
9 Quoted in P.J. Cain and A.G. Hopkins, *British Imperialism: Crisis and Deconstruction 1914–1990* (Longman, 1993), pp.218–19.
10 Holland, *European Decolonisation*, p.32.
11 Quoted in Cain and Hopkins, *British Imperialism*, p.208.
12 Quoted in Raymond F. Betts, *France and Decolonisation 1900–1960* (Macmillan, 1991), p.17.
13 Maurius Moutet, quoted in Betts, *France and Decolonisation*, p.31.
14 Ferro, *Colonization* (Routledge, 1997), p.124.
15 Quoted in Grimal, *Decolonization*, p.74.

Summary Diagram
War, Depression and Empires 1919–39

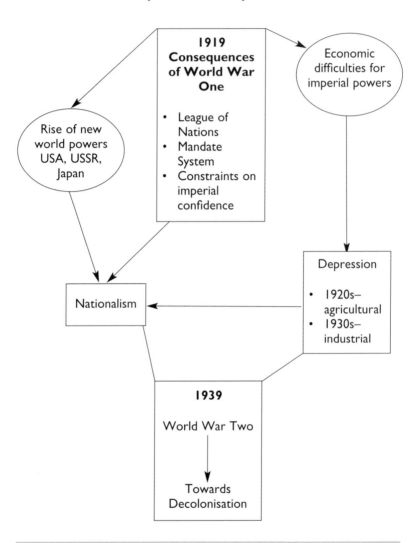

Structured questions on Chapter 2

a) What were the effects of the First World War upon the European empires? (*5 marks*)
b) What were the effects of economic depression upon them? (*5 marks*)
c) How much had the empires changed by 1939 and how predictable was decolonisation by then? Give as full a set of reasons as you can. (*10 marks*)

Hints and Advice

The method of answering a) and b) is obviously similar. You are really being asked how the two main factors, war and depression, change the empires. A key relationship examiners will want students to understand is that between continuity and change in history. So, it is worth thinking about how much change took place because of war and depression, as well as the extent to which the empires remained relatively unchanged. The factors that need considering are the degree to which the First World War weakened or strengthened empires; the effects of the Peace Settlement of 1919; the particular effects of depression upon colonial economies that were less developed than those of European ones; and the timescale of depression in the these two parts of the world.

Question c) is worth twice as many marks as a) or b), so you should organise your time accordingly to get the best overall grade you can from an examiner. This is a simple but important skill, and one that is often overlooked. Answering c) requires even more specific use of information than for a) or b). If you approach it in too general a way then it is possible to miss the fact that not all empires changed as much as others. So, distinctions need to be made between the degree of change in the British empire compared with the French and, although there is less information in this chapter on them, also compared with the Dutch, Belgian and Portuguese empires. In this way you can construct a genuinely comparative answer that demonstrates that there were different degrees of change in each empire and that it is possible to evaluate them. The final part of the question requires quite fine judgement. Predictability is perhaps a concept for statisticians rather than historians! However, it is useful here because we do want to pose questions that allow us to compare how many of the causes of decolonisation were detectable before the Second World War, before we go on to examine that war's effects in subsequent chapters. You will need to consider whether inter-war developments made any of the imperial powers less committed to retaining empires. As decolonisation also involves the activity of the colonised peoples, ask to what extent their power to change things had developed, for example through the rise of nationalism. Finally, were there any signs that other countries within the system of international relations were beginning to play a role? Could empires any longer decide their own futures independent of the views of the USA, USSR or Japan, for example? Balance out these factors and make a reasoned conclusion between them.

Source-based questions on Chapter 2

It is best to begin with some general advice on answering source-based questions. Like structured questions, they will differ from essay question in having several parts. Each part may refer to specific information. With source-based questions examiners are often looking for you to use primary sources to illuminate more general issues. So, interpret and extend the document, do not merely repeat or paraphrase it. Ask yourself whether you have delved deeper into the issue than the mere words of the document allow. Make the document speak more widely, amplify its inner meanings, but always refer back to it by way of a short reference. Remember that you should always be able to support your views from the text. Guidance questions to achieve this are: who wrote the document and why; what is the context in which it was written; are there any particularly illuminating words or phrases used; and what is the overall significance of it for the issue it has been selected to discuss? Avoid saying documents are biased, as all are to one degree or another as they are made by human beings! The examiner will want to know how this affects its usefulness and reliability as a source for the historian.

Now read the extracts on Indo-Chinese and Indonesian nationalism on pages 19 and 21 and answer the following questions. (I will give you some help with the answers this time, but in subsequent chapters there will be less.)

a) How does the Indo-Chinese document show nationalist and anti-European feelings? (*4 marks*)
b) Is the Indonesian document as confident as the Indo-Chinese one about the prospects of nationalism? (*6 marks*)
c) What do the documents show about the strengths and weaknesses of colonial nationalism in the inter-war period? (*10 marks*)

Hints and Advice

a) Quote a phrase or two here that show these feelings and most importantly, give your reasons.
b) Again, select a phrase or word that shows this document as being less confident. Give an indication of why Stalin thinks the PKI has been unsuccessful and needs to change its tactics.
c) Here you need to make a judgement about the extent to which nationalism was becoming a force to be taken account of by the colonial powers. To do this, quote from the documents and then refer relevantly to your wider knowledge about the origins of colonial nationalism and its limitations in the inter-war period. You might want to comment on whether the link between nationalism and communism could be seen as a strength or weakness.

3 British Decolonisation 1939–80

POINTS TO CONSIDER

This chapter examines the main causes and characteristics of British decolonisation. It explores the reasons why some British colonies achieved independence before others. Finally, it looks at the consequences of decolonisation for Britain and the post-colonial states.

KEY DATES

1939 Outbreak of the Second World War
1942 Fall of Singapore, Malaya and Burma to Japanese; Quit India movement
1945 End of the Second World War; Labour's election victory
1947 Indian independence
1948 British withdrawal from Palestine
1956 Suez Crisis
1957 Malay Federation created; Ghana's independence
1960 Independence of Cyprus and Nigeria; Macmillan's 'wind of change' speech
1961 Independence of Tanganyika
1962 Independence of Uganda
1963 Independence of Kenya
1964 Independence of Zambia and Malawi
1965 Rhodesian UDI
1980 Independence of Zimbabwe

1 The Effects of the Second World War

> **KEY ISSUES** How did the war change British colonialism? How did these changes affect the prospects of decolonisation after the war?

a) General factors

The war in the Far East shrunk the British Empire geographically. In 1942 the British Empire in Singapore, Malaya and Burma fell to the Japanese, who demonstrated the weakness of the old imperial power in the face of serious military challenge. In colonies like Malaya, communist-led nationalism, which had resisted the Japanese, emerged strengthened.

From 1940 war reduced the size of Britain's empire, but the colonial economies that remained were vital in confronting the enemy. In this role they developed rapidly and more independently of

Britain. But war also brought inflation to colonial economies as high wages in vital industries chased a shortage of commodity goods. The losers from inflation commonly became more receptive to nationalism.

b) Theatres of Imperial Warfare

It was from the fall of France, in June 1940, that war really began to impact upon the British Empire. The French North African Empire fell under German control, followed by Libya, a colony of her Axis partner Italy. The British Imperial and Commonwealth forces under General Montgomery halted the Axis advance at El Alamein (Egypt) in October 1942. It proved the beginning of a remarkable military reversal that resecured the Suez Canal. An Anglo-American landing in Algeria enabled the Axis to be attacked from both east and west, forcing its surrender by May 1943. The imperial war in S.E. Asia took longer to win. After war began between Japan and the United States in December 1941, the Japanese attacked the British and French empires in S.E. Asia. Singapore, Malaya and Burma all fell in 1942. But the American advance across the Pacific drew the Japanese away and enabled Britain to reclaim its former colonies by 1945.

c) Allies in Conflict over Empire

The Anglo-American Alliance was vital to Britain, yet the USA's anti-imperialism jeopardised the empire. In the Atlantic Charter (1941), President Roosevelt had justified the war to Americans as one to further democracy. Empires were not democratic, neither were they open markets. United militarily, the Allies were in diplomatic conflict. Churchill retorted, 'If Britain lost the Indian Empire ... she would sink in two generations to the rank of a minor power – like Portugal,'[1] and threatened resignation. But Churchill, for once, had misread history. Portugal clung to its empire because it was in decline as a European power. It was symptom not cause. There were more similarities than Churchill cared to acknowledge. 'I have not become His Majesty's Chief Minister to preside over the liquidation of the British Empire' he had boasted in his Mansion House speech of November 1942. But he and his successors did just that.

d) War and Imperial Decline

Holland has argued that loss of empire was symptomatic of Britain's decline after the Second World War. Post-war austerity meant that empire could no longer be subsidised. Yet, despite the economic damage of war Britain was still the world's third power. There was decline relative to the USA, but even Labour from 1945 did not see abandoning empire as the solution. It was certain specific consequences of the Second World War, not readily apparent in 1945, that led to decolonisation.

The war had severe economic consequences for empire. Concentrating upon producing munitions caused Britain to export less to the empire. These markets were often lost permanently as colonies turned to alternative suppliers, or replaced British imports with home production as India did. Munitions production in the colonies also assisted their further industrialisation.

e) India and the War

As war broke out, Congress laid out the contradictions of the British attitude. 'India ... cannot of her own free will participate in a war in defence of democracy as long as she is denied real freedom.'[2] A civil disobedience campaign followed. After the fall of France the British needed Indian support more than ever, so they offered Dominion status once the war had ended. Congress's rejection indicated that nothing short of independence would now satisfy them. Its distrust of Churchill was deepened by his excluding India from that principle of the Atlantic Charter (August 1941), which pledged 'to respect the right of all peoples to choose the form of Government under which they will live'. Churchill said later that the Charter's principles were only for Europeans. Nevertheless, he sent Sir Stafford Cripps, a Labour member of the wartime coalition, with a renewed offer of Dominion status. Gandhi dismissed it as a 'a post-dated cheque' and Nehru as one with nothing written on it. If Britain wanted Congress to support the war, immediate independence was the only way. Gandhi concluded:

> I remember that when I read these proposals for the first time I was profoundly depressed and the depression was largely due to the fact that I had expected something more substantial from Sir Stafford Cripps as well as from the critical situation that had arisen. When analysed
> 5 there were so many limitations, and the very principle of self-determination was fettered and circumscribed in such a way as to imperil our future.[3]

Congress divided over how best to deal with the British.

> Gandhi now turned his mind to the need to find an appropriate response to the failure of the mission. Within days of the breakdown he was seized and increasingly consumed by the idea which came to him ... that the British should quit India at once and thus lessen the risk of
> 5 a Japanese invasion.[4]

But Congress President, Subhas Chandra Bose, disagreed with Gandhi's *satyagraha* (non-violent resistance), and led the breakaway Indian National Army in armed struggle. It fought with the Japanese against the British in Burma and set up a 'free Indian Government' in Singapore.

Gandhi argued that 'Britain cannot defend India, much less herself on Indian soil with any strength.' The war, he thought, would result in nothing less than the defeat of imperialism throughout Asia. In the short-term, 'Quit India' weakened Congress because its leaders were interned. Its lost momentum allowed the growth of its rival the Muslim League. The Viceroy, Lord Linlithgow, exacerbated the situation by using the League to undermine Congress. The League, under its leader Jinnah, had been arguing for partition since 1940. Congress, Hindu-dominated but a multi-religious party, opposed separatism as absurd. Gandhi asked, should they have other separate nations for Sikhs and Parsis when they were all of one race?

Inflation, food shortages and then famine in 1943–44 further damaged Anglo-Indian relations because the British were accused of looking on. At the Simla Conference (June 1945), Linlithgow's replacement Lord Wavell failed to get agreement on the recycled Cripps proposals designed to produce a Congress-Muslim League coalition. The war in Europe ended with Indians united that British rule must end, but divided over what should succeed it. The British government was increasingly coming round to Wavell's view that India had become ungovernable. Churchill's wartime policy of holding on by any ploy was no longer tenable. Economically, there were also strong reasons for contemplating withdrawal. War demand had accelerated Indian industrialisation, strengthening the position of businessmen represented in the Congress Party. India's financial position was transformed from debtor into creditor of Britain. Although Lancashire textile manufacturers saw their Indian markets disappear by 1945, the 'gentlemanly capitalists' of the City had got their money back with interest.

f) The Effects of War upon British Africa

Firstly, the war led to economic development. The campaign to grow more food stimulated the rural economy and raised living standards. Transferring war production to Africa stimulated industrialisation and avoided possible destruction of plant in Europe. Urban growth continued after the war and produced a more politically conscious population.

Secondly, war resulted in more direct control by the imperialist state. The Colonial Development and Welfare Act of 1940 promised an investment programme designed to keep the colonies loyal through the war. Little was actually done, which was why its critics condemned it as window dressing for international opinion. Wartime shortages and inflation caused a build-up of discontent already present amongst a middle class suffering frustrated career opportunities. The result was the Hailey Report, held back until 1944 because of its controversial restatement of the aims of colonial government. It recommended better education for Africans to enable progress towards self-government. But this, in itself, created further problems, as Hargreaves outlines:

1   educational expansion ... aroused the greatest African enthusiasm, and the highest expectations. There were more expectations than could be quickly satisfied. Many administrators thought that Higher Education received too high priority from Colonial Office planners, especially
5   when they realized how heavily those planners had underestimated the costs of a modern university. But this view was rarely shared by Africans, who saw university degrees as master keys to national progress ... At every level of the educational pyramid queues of disappointed aspirants began to form.[5]

Thirdly, war weakened colonial administrations and strengthened the position of white settlers in their strongholds in East Africa. As bureaucrats were called up to serve in the armed forces, white settlers replaced them in colonial government, a role they hoped to retain after the war.

Fourthly, the war strengthened the South African economy, the most industrialised in Africa. By so doing, it strengthened the emerging politics of racial segregation in that region. South Africa later helped resist decolonisation in Southern Rhodesia and the Portuguese colonies. Both this fourth effect, and the third, were factors retarding decolonisation, whereas the first and second tended to accelerate it.

2 Britain's Imperial Situation in 1945

> **KEY ISSUES** How did Britain's changed post-war condition affect the empire? How did the new system of international relations do so? To what extent had the war strengthened colonial nationalism?

a) The British Economy

As the war ended the British economy was squeezed from two directions. On the one hand, war loans had turned it from a creditor into a debtor. On the other, the impending Cold War called for high levels of defence spending. But instead of reducing costs by decolonising, governments decided to make the colonies more economically efficient. This policy of 'new imperialism' was designed to produce both cheap food and export earnings. But it clashed with two forces encouraging decolonisation. The first was the increased economic independence enjoyed by many colonies during the war. The second was the emerging body of British opinion that thought formal imperialism had become unnecessary. These included 'neo-colonialists' who admired American global exploitation of free markets, and those who wanted to replace empire with a common European market.

However, immediately after the war, British governments showed no preference for either option. The City of London urged continued commitment to formal empire and the Sterling Area. Only from the late 1950s was there a turn to Europe.

b) British Politics

Labour's election victory of 1945 was not a fundamental cause of decolonisation. Although many *socialists* were anti-imperialists, many Labour politicians were committed to empire, and it was Labour that presided over the first stages of the 'new imperialism'. It was the Labour Foreign Secretary, Ernest Bevin, who declared 'our crime is not exploitation; it's neglect'.[6] Bevin has been criticised for failing to appreciate that imperialism had become incompatible with the modernisation of British politics. The 'march of democracy' had to involve decolonisation. Others took a more pragmatic view and argued that empire had to be sacrificed in order to afford a universal welfare state.

c) International Relations

The Second World War relegated Britain to the second division of world powers. The emergence of the United States as leader of the West influenced whether British imperialism was to continue. The USA wanted to trade freely throughout the world. It disliked the way in which Britain protected its empire through the Sterling Area. However, US foreign policy had also to take account of the other superpower, the USSR. Neither the USA nor Britain wanted decolonisation to result in communist expansion. A compromise was therefore reached. The USA did not pressurise Britain to decolonise where it was likely to lead to communism gaining power. Only pro-western governments should be permitted to replace colonial ones.

d) The Rise of Nationalism

Post-war circumstances strengthened nationalism and fitted it to play a powerful role in decolonisation. Firstly, the 'new imperialism' taxed colonised peoples more heavily. Secondly, indirect rule through local chiefs was in decline as political leadership passed into the hands of the urban middle classes. Thirdly, the colonial bureaucracies, run down and weakened during the war, were forced to open up government as nationalist movements pressed for inclusion.

3 British Decolonisation in Asia

KEY ISSUE Why did India decolonise so rapidly and Malaya so slowly after the Second World War?

a) India

The new Labour government of July 1945 took Viceroy Wavell's advice to seek to establish a unitary state under Congress leadership. But the violence that followed the Muslim League's rejection forced them to compromise. In February 1946, Cripps again unsuccessfully sought a federal settlement that would satisfy Muslim separatism. By then, even Congress leaders accepted that Jinnah would settle for nothing less than a sovereign Pakistan, to include most of the Punjab and Bengal (the north-western and north-eastern regions where there were Muslim majorities). In August, serious rioting occurred in Bengal when an interim Congress-Muslim League government collapsed. Wavell was withdrawn from India in February 1947, as mass violence threatened to consume his administration. His replacement, Lord Mountbatten, had served in India during the war. He was instructed by Prime Minister Attlee to bring about Britain's withdrawal by June 1948. Twelve months ahead of time, he produced a plan that would achieve this through partition. There were to be two dominions of India and Pakistan, and each province was to choose which to join. Because the Muslim population was concentrated in the north-west and north-east, Pakistan would be in two parts separ-

Victims of riots, New Delhi 1947

ated by a thousand miles. Punjab and Bengal, which had Muslim majorities but substantial non-Muslim minorities, were to be partitioned. Furthermore, Mountbatten brought forward the date of dominion status to 15 August 1947, almost a year in advance of the original proposal.

Mountbatten's acceleration of the decolonisation timetable left Congress and the Muslim League jostling for position. In the process, the interests of minority groups such as the Sikhs were neglected. There was also the problem of the princely states. These were ruled over by rich landowners who recognised British authority but were not officially part of the empire. They constituted 80 million people and one-third of the land mass, yet Mountbatten made no provision for them in the settlement. Eventually, through a combination of pressure and promises that guaranteed the continuation of their titles and landownership, the princely states joined with India. Appalling inter-communal violence followed partition, especially in the areas with mixed religious populations. A mass migration took place of people fleeing for the safe side of the frontier. Killings continued for months after independence. Gandhi was an uncompromising critic of religious murder. On 30 January 1948, as he walked to evening prayers in Delhi, he was shot three times by a Hindu fanatic who favoured it. Indian decolonisation had claimed its most ironic victim. A pacifist advocate of religious unity had died at the hands of a sectarian gunman of his own religion.

Historians disagree over the wisdom of the rapidity of India's decolonisation. One view argues that much of the inter-communal violence could have been anticipated and minimised if the Labour Government had not conspired with Mountbatten to leave as soon as possible. This is a grave charge, for over a million people lost their lives between 1947 and 1948, and 13 million were made refugees. Others take the opposite view, that swift withdrawal was sensible and saved lives. Holland credits Mountbatten for recognising the inevitability of partition and getting on with the job. The longer it took, he thinks, the more lives it would have cost. Darwin, more concerned with the effects upon British foreign policy, praises Mountbatten for a settlement that kept both new states inside the Commonwealth, and appeased both the Muslim world and the USA. Such judgements are difficult, for the historian's main task is to explain what *did* happen rather than what might have happened. However, there is no doubt that the settlement of June 1947 did not begin the violence. It was already occurring as communities insecure over the possible 'Balkanisation' of the sub-continent turned against each other. Mountbatten was more trusted by Indian leaders than the previous Viceroy. He was seen as someone who would better balance Indian and British interests. India went on to join the Commonwealth as a republic in 1948, thereby setting a precedent for many other decolonised nations. Pakistan followed suit in 1955.

Indian decolonisation was little opposed in Britain. An important explanation is that 'In Britain's changed and desperate economic situation in 1945, India had ceased to be an imperial asset.'[7] Between the wars, India had declined as a market for British exports, while imports had increased. Britain's modest trade surplus with India of the 1920s had turned into a deficit by the 1930s. The deficit was worsened by the boycotting of British goods. However, by that time the key British interest in India was not manufacturing, but finance. The City did not mind if India traded beyond Britain provided it paid back its loans. This it continued to do precisely because it found new export markets. From 1945, the Labour government's priorities did not lie in India. American aid was needed for post-war reconstruction, the

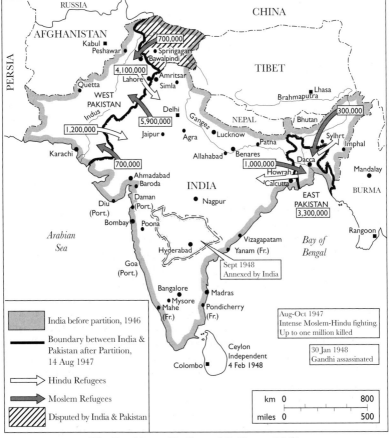

The Partition of India and Pakistan, 1947

Welfare State, and to patrol the Iron Curtain. Given these economic reasons behind Indian decolonisation, Labour and Mountbatten were able to play an accelerating political role.

b) Malaya

In Malaya's ethnically divided society, the Chinese community was slightly larger than the Malay. The Indian community was only about one-third the size of the other two. The Malayan Peoples' Anti-Japanese Army led the resistance and was in a strong position in 1945. It was Chinese and communist-dominated. It disarmed because the British promised equal rights for the Chinese community.

Britain delayed Malayan decolonisation for several reasons. Malayan tin and rubber exports were valuable dollar earners that could help pay off Britain's war debts. Strategically, Singapore was the gateway to East Asia for both trade and defence. Politically, the Malayan archipelago was a complicated entity. It was composed of different types of territories: crown colonies like Singapore, that were administered directly from London; and Malay States, protectorates with Commissioners working in close collaboration with local Sultans.

From its foundation in 1946, the United Malays' National Organisation successfully prevented the British from introducing equal rights for Chinese and Indians. A federal constitution (1948) preserved the Sultan's powers. In protest, angry young Chinese males volunteered for the communist, guerrilla training camps in the jungle. Chinese farmers supplied these 'liberated areas'. But the Indian community rejected communism as 'Chinese.' Trade unionism recruited amongst the working class of Kuala Lumpur and the dockers of Singapore.

Malayan communists thought that Indian decolonisation showed Britain had lost its commitment to remain an imperial power. But this did not take account of Cold War politics. Britain resisted any decolonisation that would let in communism. In June 1948, the murder of three British planters by communists led to the declaration of an Emergency (martial law). But there were insufficient troops to police it effectively. A change of policy set up resettlement communities for rural squatters. These eventually held one quarter of the Chinese community. In 1952, an anti-insurgency campaign gave guerrillas amnesty if they would agree to be 're-educated'. The communist insurrection petered out.

The Chinese community divided over communism along class lines. Business people opposed it and formed the Malayan Chinese Association. The MCA persuaded the Malays in UMNO to open up the bureaucracy to Chinese. In 1953, the two parties formed an alliance with the Malayan Indian Congress. This coalition won the 1955 elections and formed the first government of the newly independent Malay Federation. The communist insurrection had taught the Malay ruling class the necessity for ethnic co-operation. The multi-ethnic coalition government represented the elites, with whom the British continued on good terms. Agreement was reached on the retention of key military bases. But harmony did not prevail within the Federation. The new, expanded state of Malaysia (1963) reasserted Malay dominance, with British complicity. By that time, however, the communist threat had diminished.

Malayan decolonisation is full of paradoxes. Initial British intentions to create more equality rebounded and caused a guerrilla war. Communist revolt was ethnic rather than class based and retarded decolonisation rather than accelerated it. The slowness of decolonisation is explained not only by ethnic politics, but also by Cold War considerations. After China in 1949 and Indo-China in 1954, Malaya could not be allowed to be the next Asian domino to fall to communism.

4 Suez: the Turning-point of Decolonisation?

> **KEY ISSUE** Why is Suez seen as the turning-point in British decolonisation?

a) Invasion

On 29 October 1956, Israel invaded her neighbour Egypt. Britain and France had put her up to the attack and supported it by bombing Egyptian airfields and landing troops along the Suez Canal. The action met with almost universal condemnation from the international community, including the United States. Britain and France had to withdraw and a United Nations force was put in to separate Egyptians and Israelis. How had British policy proved capable of such a disastrous misjudgement?

b) Long-term origins

The Treaty of Versailles (1919) had granted Britain a mandate over Palestine, out of the territory of the defeated Turkish Empire. Two years before, the Balfour Declaration had supported the historic rights of Jews:

1 His Majesty's Government view with favour the establishment in Palestine of a national home for the Jewish people, and will use their best endeavours to facilitate this object, it being clearly understood that nothing shall be done that shall prejudice the civil and religious rights of
5 the existing non-Jewish communities in Palestine.[8]

Balfour stopped short of supporting an exclusively Jewish state in

Palestine. Jewish immigration was allowed to increase through the 1930s, but was reduced during the war because Britain needed the goodwill of the Arab states. However, the Holocaust strengthened the case for a Jewish homeland. Britain gave up its Mandate to the UNO, which approved partition of Palestine (November 1947), and the British withdrew in May 1948. The victory of the Israelis in the subsequent war against the Arabs resulted in a much bigger state than the UNO had sanctioned. It also created around 700,000 homeless, Palestinian Arab, refugees. The Arab states held Britain primarily responsible for allowing this to happen. They blamed Britain for not imposing a multi-racial state in Palestine that would have reflected the Arab majority in the region.

c) Short-term origins

Egypt was one of the defeated Arab states that held Britain to blame. Terrorism against British bases developed. In 1952 a group of officers overthrew the old, feudal monarchy of King Faruk. Gamal Abdel Nasser emerged as their leader and President by 1956. Nasser's pan-Arabism wanted to unite all Arab states against imperialism. The British recruited allies from client Middle Eastern regimes in the Baghdad Pact (1955). Nasser condemned this as neo-colonialism. Egyptian and British foreign policies were on opposing paths. Although never a communist, Nasser agreed with the USSR that the common enemy was western imperialism. This explains Soviet support for Egypt in the war of 1956. Harold Macmillan, who supported the invasion, thought he saw in Nasser a different type of post-colonial leader and lamented 'the collapse of the agreeable, educated, Liberal, North Oxford society to whom we have transferred power.'[9] In July 1956, Nasser nationalised the Suez Canal, vital to Britain's trade and oil supplies. He felt let down by the World Bank's withdrawal from financing the Aswan Dam project his country needed. He was also annoyed by Britain's failure to give up their military base along the Suez Canal, as agreed in 1954. These immediate grievances, however, should be placed in the long-term context of Arab mistrust of British behaviour in the Middle East.

d) Suez and decolonisation

As Egypt had been independent since 1922, how did Suez affect decolonisation? Suez was a victory for Egyptian nationalism and a boost for Third World confidence. Britain had been caught behaving like an old imperialist power in a world that would no longer tolerate it. It proved the end of its serious influence in the Middle East, and confirmed its decline as an imperial power. Further withdrawals from East of Suez were to follow. The British government had to restore relations with the Commonwealth. India had threatened to leave over

Two views of Suez:

1 Cartoon from the *Daily Express*.

2 A Russian comment on the Suez fiasco.

Suez. The affair had thrown the special relationship with the USA into doubt. Suez had caused a run on the pound that the Americans refused to help staunch. Britain was left to pay the price for its imperial escapade. It caused the resignation of the humiliated Prime Minister, Eden, the next year. His successor, Macmillan, steered the Conservatives towards accepting decolonisation.

5 British Decolonisation in Africa

KEY ISSUES Why did British decolonisation in Africa begin later than in Asia and then proceed so rapidly? What were the differences between decolonisation in West, East, Central and Southern Africa? What effects did the Cold War have?

a) The Wind of Change

In February 1960, Macmillan told a South African parliament he was eager to educate:

> The most striking of all the impressions I have formed since I left London a month ago is of the strength of ... African national consciousness. In different places it may take different forms. But it is happening everywhere. The wind of change is blowing through this Continent.[10]

Yet in 1945 there had scarcely been a breeze. By the mid-1960s Macmillan's metaphor was too moderate to describe the hurricane of decolonisation that swept across British Africa. Nigeria followed Ghana to independence in 1960, Tanganyika and Sierra Leone in 1961, Uganda in 1962, Kenya in 1963, Zambia and Malawi in 1964, The Gambia in 1965, Botswana and Lesotho in 1966, Swaziland and Mauritius in 1968.

Darwin locates the eye of the storm in 'the economics of decline'. By the late 1950s the Sterling Area was no longer doing its job of protecting Britain from American competition. The value of the primary goods most of its members produced had fallen. Waites, however, amasses more convincing evidence that colonial economies grew after 1945. He argues that decolonisation was more 'a revolution of rising expectations'. Not in doubt is that British investment in colonial markets was less profitable than in Europe and elsewhere. The 1950s was a decade of enormous growth in the British economy on which the 'new imperialism' was a blemish.

When political arguments were added, the case for decolonisation became stronger. Iain Macleod was Colonial Secretary in Macmillan's government from 1959. He explained decolonisation in this way:

> 1 The situation in autumn, 1959 was grim ... It has been said that after I became Colonial Secretary there was a deliberate speeding up of the movement towards independence. I agree. There was. And in my view any other policy would have led to terrible bloodshed in Africa ... we
> 5 could not possibly have held by force our territories in Africa ... The march of men towards freedom can be guided, but not halted.[11]

So, for Macleod, astute political leadership able to guide irresistible historical forces is very important. John F. Kennedy, who became President of the United States in January 1961, agreed and also favoured decolonisation in Africa.

b) From the Gold Coast to Ghana

Ghana's relatively peaceful transition to independence and initial political stability caused it to be held up as a model of decolonisation. This might not have been predicted in February 1948, when the capital city of Accra erupted into riots. One cause of these riots lay in the 'new imperialist' policy of extracting more economic growth from the colonies. Cocoa producers complained at the mass lopping of diseased cocoa trees. In the towns, middle-class youth led protests against continuing wartime controls, rising unemployment and inflation. Another cause lay in the 1946 Constitution that gave the rural chiefs more power on the Legislative Council than the urban classes.

In 1948 the Cold War had just begun. Unsettled by the communist coup in Czechoslovakia, the British arrested Kwame Nkrumah on suspicion of being an ideological ally of Moscow. Nkrumah, general secretary of the United Gold Coast Convention, was a nationalist but not a communist. He was born in 1909 and had been educated in the United States and Britain. Prison radicalised him. On release he broke with the United Gold Coast Convention and founded the Convention People's Party (1949). The CPP appealed to discontented urban groups and smaller cocoa growers over the heads of the rural chiefs who collaborated with colonialism. But the chiefs themselves were discontented with the higher taxes of the 'new imperialism' that ate into their cocoa profits.

The Coussey Committee (1949) proposed self-government but under the control of the chiefs. The CPP spread into a mass party, galvanising anti-colonial opinion. Elections under the new, Coussey Constitition enabled the CPP to win a large majority in the national assembly in 1951. Nkrumah had to be released from prison. He campaigned on the slogan of 'Self-government NOW' forcing the British to shape an acceptable timetable towards independence. The Colonial Secretary, Oliver Lyttelton, voiced Cold War concerns when he told the British Government that the Gold Coast Cabinet had agreed

> 1   to ban the entry of all Communist literature into the Gold Coast ... to exclude any European with Communist sympathies from the public service and to exclude any African with Communist sympathies from a certain number of Departments like the Administration, the police and
> 5   the Department of education ... to confiscate the passports of the few Gold Coast Communists who wish to travel behind the Iron Curtain.[12]

Nkrumah's good relationship with the Governor, Arden-Clarke, eased a smooth transition to independence in the face of growing opposition from disaffected cocoa growers in the North. The CPP's stronghold was in the South, but revived cocoa prices quietened the North. In 1954, the administration called fresh elections. The CPP won again but with a reduced majority, losing control of the North. The Northern opposition then united with the discontented cocoa growers of the Ashanti region to form the National Liberation Movement. The NLM wanted to keep power regional in a federal state, unlike the CPP which wanted a unitary one.

Arden-Clarke supported Nkrumah as the best bet for a peaceful transition to independence and the CPP won another electoral victory in 1957. It had overcome the opposition to emerge a national party ready to manage the transition to nationhood. The new Ghana of March 1957 was a unitary state, and federalists had to be satisfied with regional assemblies. British propaganda presented Ghana as a model of decolonisation, but the model soon had egg on its face as Ghana became a one-party state. Macmillan made his 'wind of change' speech first in Accra, before going on to Cape Town. By that time a Cold War wind was blowing on Britain as Ghana leaned towards the USSR.

Hit by a two-thirds fall in world cocoa prices in the 1960s Nkrumah's regime became increasingly dictatorial. He was over-thrown by a military coup in 1966. The succeeding military leaders did nothing to lessen the corruption Nkrumah had allowed. Thus, Flight Lieutenant Jerry Rawlings led a further coup in 1979 commit-ted to reduce it. He improved the economy through the 1980s, reduc-ing inflation and obtaining investment from the West. In 1992 constitutional government was restored and Rawlings was elected President in 1996 for the first time.

c) Nigeria

Nigerian decolonisation was more difficult than Ghanaian because of deeper ethnic and religious divisions. The north was Muslim and ruled over by feudal landowners of the Fulani tribe. The South was predominantly Christian, but tribally divided between the Yoruba in the west and the Igbos in the east. Regionalism undermined nation-alism. The first party to call itself nationalist, the National Council of Nigeria and the Cameroons (1944), was in fact regional and Igbo dominated. Nigeria did not have a strong nationalist middle class like Ghana's despite the western seaboard being commercially developed. The 1951 elections saw two more regional parties emerge: the Action Group representing the Yoruba and the Northern People's Congress representing the Northern Muslims. The British felt the only hope of creating a nation state out of divided Nigeria was to concede full regional autonomy. This was promised in the revised constitution of 1954.

The first government after independence in 1960 was a fragile Muslim–Igbo coalition. The Yoruba went into opposition. Co-oper-ation lasted only until the discovery of oil and gas deposits in the early 1960s set off competition for the proceeds. Army coups between 1964 and 1966 endeavoured to hold together the central state. But the Igbos in the East suffered and broke away as Biafra in 1967. A terrible three-year civil war defeated this secession. The Army has remained the power behind Nigerian politics ever since. The state has survived, but in a fractured condition that military rule has only suppressed not cured. Through the 1990s, an elite of Nigerian generals in league with multinational companies monopolised precious oil resources.

They ravaged the local environment of Ogoniland and executed opponents. Decolonisation has not delivered a stable, peaceful state in Nigeria, which has only recently returned to democracy.

JULIUS NYERERE (1922–99)

Pan-African and first President of Tanzania

-*Profile*-

Tanzanian decolonisation can be approached through a remarkable personal history.

Tanganyika was a German colony before becoming a British mandate in 1919. When it became a UN trustee territory in 1946, Britain accepted obligations to advance it towards self-rule. This proceeded smoothly largely because there were no white settlers' interests to take account of. Another reason was the creation of a united nationalist party, the Tanganyikan African National Union (ZANU), by an exceptional leader, Julius Nyerere.

Nyerere did not attend school until he was twelve. From then, he thrived under the teaching of Catholic priests whose religion he kept all his life in predominantly Muslim Tanganyika. He was the first Tanganyikan to win a scholarship to a British university. He went to Edinburgh in 1949, at a time when Britain had a Labour Government. His studies led him to consider how his socialism might be applied to Africa. Returning to Tanganyika as a schoolteacher, he reluctantly gave it up to found ZANU in 1954. He was always referred to by his people as *mwalimu*, the teacher. In 1958, he was one of the first Africans to be elected to the Legislature. He rose to chief minister in 1960, and became independent Tanganyika's first Prime Minister in 1961. The country united with Zanzibar as Tanzania in 1964.

Nyerere's importance to the history of decolonisation extends across Africa. He demonstrated this Pan-Africanism through deeds, not merely words. Nyerere played a key role in the defeat of Portuguese colonialism, and of white rule in both Rhodesia and South Africa. He took pride in being called the 'evil genius' behind guerrilla liberation movements by the white Rhodesian leader Ian Smith. Frelimo (Mozambique), the Patriotic Front (Rhodesia), and the ANC (South Africa), were all given bases in Tanzania. On the other hand, he became the first post-colonial,

African leader to violate the Organisation of African Unity's rules by invading another country, when his armies helped Ugandan exiles topple the Amin regime in 1978–9. His embarrassment was eased by Ugandans in Kampala chanting his name as the Tanzanian armies rolled in.

Within Tanzania, Nyerere tried to build African socialism. The state almost completely replaced private enterprise. His greatest failure lay in the communal agricultural system, known as *ujamaa* (familyhood), which was resisted by local village and district heads. The oil crisis of the early 1970s raised Tanzania's import bill so high that it had nothing left for basic investment. In one of African history's most ironic tragedies, he stepped down as President in 1985 leaving the country whose independence he had fathered more deeply indebted to foreign aid than any other in Africa.

d) Uganda

As in Nigeria, tribal separatism in Uganda strongly impeded national unification. But there was no significant white settler class to appease, as there was in neighbouring Kenya. The most powerful tribe, the Buganda, feared being merged into a unitary state. The British tried to pacify them by granting regional autonomy. In 1962, the Buganda were cajoled into accepting an independent, unitary state under the Uganda People's Congress led by Milton Obote.

Uganda has had a turbulent, post-colonial history. Bugandan separatism survived independence and Obote used the army against it in 1966. Obote was, himself, overthrown by Idi Amin in 1971. His military dictatorship terrorised opposition and expelled the 70,000 strong Asian community. Amin's rule was only ended by the Tanzanian invasion of 1978. Uganda did not recover until the 1990s from the economic bankruptcy inflicted upon it by Amin's corrupt rule. After 1985, the Museveni government restored democracy, but Uganda remains a desperately poor country.

e) Kenya

In Kenya a large white settler population dominated landholding. In the fertile 'White Highlands', Africans were restricted to overcrowded tribal reserves, where they were impoverished. At the end of the war the Governor, Sir Philip Mitchell, suggested land reform for Africans. Whites, strengthened on the Legislative Council during the war, opposed financing this out of taxes. African nationalism, minimally organised before the war, found a voice in the Kenyan African Union (founded 1944), which accused the whites of 'land theft'. It was led by

Jomo Kenyatta of the dominant Kikuyu tribe. He was born in 1891. Educated in a Church of Scotland Mission and baptised a Christian, he became politically active in the 1920s while a government clerk in Nairobi. As secretary of the Kikuyu Central Association, he championed Kikuyu land rights. He later studied anthropology in London, which resulted in his book *Facing Mount Kenya* (1938). As president of KAU at the beginning of the Mau Mau rebellion, he was falsely accused of being its instigator and imprisoned until 1961.

In 1950, the administration gave way to demands from white farmers to ban the KAU. This encouraged Africans' discontents to fester as their political activity was driven into secrecy. These were the origins of the movement known as Mau Mau, whose aim was to restore Africans to their historic lands. But it also had support in the urban areas, where there had been a post-war decline in living standards. White fears were deepened by the oath taking that was traditional amongst the Kikuyu:

> In official eyes, and even more in the minds of the settlers, Mau Mau was not the articulation of grievance and fear but a barbaric throwback ... held together by the use of oaths of 'unspeakable debauchery', playing upon the lowest and most primeval instincts.[13]

The political violence in Kenya (1952–56) that led to London declaring an Emergency has been interpreted as a three-dimensional civil war. Firstly, there was the black-white conflict. Secondly, there was fighting between the Kikuyu and other tribes. Thirdly, there was fighting within the Kikuyu themselves. Because far more blacks were killed than whites, the second and third can be judged most important. Mau Mau attacked blacks it accused of collaborating, such as chieftains given land by the administration. Other tactics such as cattle maiming and arson aroused white prejudices about 'dark age' behaviour. But most historians now emphasise the modern nature of the revolt. Although it employed traditional forms of protest, it was based upon economic grievances. Hargreaves describes Mau Mau as 'a tribally-based peasant revolt originally formed on the fringe of a nationalist movement'.[14]

Mau Mau was contained by a combination of repression and reform. Camps were set up to 'rehabilitate' activists. Troops and police suppressed unrest in key centres like Nairobi. On the other hand, the Swynnerton Plan (1954) helped Africans buy land. It aimed to create a class of smallholders with an interest in social stability. Africans and Asians were allowed to sit on the Legislative Council for the first time. Political parties were legalised again in 1955, and more Africans enfranchised in 1956. By 1957, Africans had equal representation with Europeans on the Legislative Council. Thus, the crushing of Mau Mau had actually led to long-delayed improvements for Africans.

By the time the Lancaster House Conference met in London in

1959, two new social forces accelerated decolonisation. The first was the rise of Kenyan trade unionism. The second was the New Kenya Group. The NKG were white businessmen whose companies ran large farms. They wanted a negotiated settlement with African politicians to protect these. Independent white farmers began to desert the Highlands as land values plummeted. The British Government compensated returning whites with help from the World Bank. As Macmillan said, 'settlement has been aristocratic and upper middle class (much more than Rhodesia) and has strong links with the City and the Clubs.'[15] Black labourers left unemployed in the Highlands were resettled.

After Kenyatta was released from prison, KAU joined the government and participated in the second Lancaster House Conference of 1962. Once independence had been promised for December 1963, KAU accepted a federalist constitution. Kenyatta was elected the first Prime Minister of an independent Kenya and became President the following year. Thus, Kenya joined Tanzania and Uganda as independent states in East Africa. After the violence of Mau Mau, this had ultimately been achieved peacefully. Under Kenyatta and his successor Daniel Arap Moi, Kenya became a one-party state. In the opinion of Ogot and Zeleza '... decolonization marked a turbulent transition from a settler dominated economy to an independent nation under an indigenous ruling class ... getting more widely and firmly integrated into the world capitalist system.'[16]

f) Central and Southern Africa

i) The Central African Federation (1953–63)

The CAF was created because Britain wanted to make a single, viable colony out of the protectorates of Nyasaland, Northern Rhodesia, and the self-governing colony of Southern Rhodesia. The idea was to smooth out Nyasaland's economic backwardness through federation with the copper-rich Northern Rhodesia and the agriculturally prosperous, industrialising Southern Rhodesia. But the territories were racially different. Nyasaland was almost exclusively black. Northern Rhodesia had a small, white settler class, who ran the copper industry. Southern Rhodesia had a larger, white population; most were farmers, but there was also an urban middle and working class. Whites had had effective self-government since 1923. They sought independence to preserve racial segregation from blacks.

Dr. Hastings Banda, leader of the Nyasaland National Congress, voiced African criticism of the CAF. It was a device to preserve white control, not to create 'partnership'. In 1959, the Devlin Commission also condemned it as a police state for imprisoning hundreds of nationalists, including Banda, after disturbances. Northern Rhodesia was little better. The Monckton Commission (1960) hastened the

CAF's demise by condemning racial rule, singling-out Southern Rhodesia for particular criticism.

Harold Macmillan returned from his 'wind of change' visit to Africa convinced that the Conservative Party had to embrace decolonisation. Nyasaland left the CAF as soon as blacks obtained a majority on the Legislative Council (July 1960). Independence, as Malawi, followed in July 1964. Northern Rhodesia followed a similar path. Multi-racial elections imposed from London in 1962 led the black dominated government to leave the Federation. The new Zambia became independent in October 1964.

ii) Southern Rhodesia and the Origins of Zimbabwe

Decolonisation in Southern Rhodesia proved far more difficult. To the whites the British government's 'wind of change' policy shift was a betrayal by their own 'kith and kin'. They wanted decolonisation, but under white rule. Their siege mentality resulted in the ultra-conservative Rhodesian Front being elected in 1962. Ian Smith became Prime Minister in April 1964. He proved a master strategist in his dealings with Harold Wilson, the British Prime Minister. Smith's Unilateral Declaration of Independence on 11 November 1965 followed a tactical error by the British Government.

> ı Before Smith's October visit to London, the Rhodesian leader had been
> moving towards independence uncertainly, with one area of lingering
> doubt – the possible use by the British Government of military force.
> According to Flower [his Secret Service chief] his self-assurance visibly
> 5 improved after his return to Salisbury, apparently because he had been
> told in London that the British did not consider the use of force 'prac-
> tical politics'.[17]

Wilson feared a mutiny if the British Army, many of whom sympathised with UDI, were asked to fight the well-trained and equipped Rhodesian army. Instead, the black nationalist organisations were left to do the fighting. Economic sanctions were not well supported. Rhodesia already had the most diversified economy in Africa. It was lubricated by South African oil through the Mozambican pipeline controlled by the Portuguese. This strengthened Smith's hand in the two rounds of failed negotiations aboard HMS *Tiger* (1966) and HMS *Fearless* (1968).

Edward Heath's Conservative Government (1970–4) established the Pearce Commission (1972) which reported that Africans rejected the phasing-in of majority rule over several decades. Both the Heath and Wilson governments tried compromises unacceptable to black Africans. In any case, the Zimbabwean African National Union (ZANU) and the Zimbabwean African People's Union (ZAPU) launched guerrilla warfare against the Smith government in 1964. Their leaders, Robert Mugabe and Josuah Nkomo, spent long periods as political prisoners of the Rhodesian regime.

The nationalists operated initially from Zambia. Portuguese decolonisation transformed their prospects. Firstly, ZANU obtained a second front in Mozambique from its Marxist ally FRELIMO. It lived off the land and won over the peasantry as Mao's Red Army had done in China. Secondly, FRELIMO cut off Rhodesia's oil pipeline. Cold War considerations also came into play. Neither the USA, nor South Africa or Zambia wanted ZANU to lead a Marxist Rhodesia into a band of such states spread across the centre of Africa. Smith had to negotiate with the black leaders for the first time in 1975. Stalemate caused ZANU-ZAPU to unite in the Patriotic Front (PF) in 1976 and step up the guerrilla war.

By 1979 the Rhodesian economy was wilting. Smith reached an 'internal settlement' with 'moderate' black leaders that produced Bishop Abel Muzorewa as Prime Minister in a white controlled political system that preserved their land ownership. The Commonwealth Conference condemned it as a puppet government because the PF refused to participe in the elections. It insisted on all-party elections monitored for fairness. All parties agreed to this at the Lancaster House Conference (September 1979). Lord Carrington, Foreign Secretary in the Thatcher Government, did not want to transfer power to the Marxist Mugabe. But this policy, nicknamed 'ABM' (Anyone But Mugabe), lay in ruins once ZANU won the February 1980 elections. But Mugabe could be constrained. If he changed the constitution within seven years of independence or confiscated property without full compensation, British and US aid would be stopped.

Zimbabwe (April 1980) was created painfully out of a long colonial war that damaged much of Southern and Central Africa. In Britain, racist attitudes within the British electorate, parties and the Army held back majority rule. But the PF and the black Commonwealth would accept nothing less. It was ironic that the Thatcher government, apartheid's best friend, presided over Rhodesian decolonisation. How do we explain this? It is a good example of changing international relations forcing a decolonisation. Portugal's withdrawal from Africa by 1975 reminded Europe that it lost colonial wars. White Rhodesia could not survive surrounded by black governments, with waning support from South Africa, and none at all from the USA. Even Carrington was reconciled to creating the most moderate black government.

In 1987, ZANU and ZAPU merged into ZANU-PF to form a one-party state. Like many African states Zimbabwe argues this diminishes tribal rivalries. It also consolidated President Mugabe's power. His government began moderate land redistribution in 1992, once the constitutional provisions protecting white land ownership had expired. By 2000, corruption within the ZANU-PF elite, violent and illegal land occupations, and economic depression brought on by involvement in the Congo's civil war, led to a Movement for

Democratic Change narrowly losing the election. Zimbabwe had evolved a volatile multi-party politics.

g) Assessment

British decolonisation in Africa was strikingly rapid. Darwin notes, '... in the middle of 1959 most of the important questions about the shape of decolonisation in Africa remained open. Less than four years later almost everything had been resolved'[18] Suez is seen as a turning-point because it caused the 'wind of change' but it only accelerated changes already underway since the 1940s.

African decolonisation was merged into the Cold War. The USA and the USSR influenced the outcomes of decolonisations. Because the Cold War deepened between 1950 and 1980, later decolonisations like Rhodesia were more embroiled in such conflicts than earlier ones such as Ghana.

Decolonisation was an uneven process. Within each colony, specifics determined the precise nature of the outcome. For example, tribalism could prevent both national unity and socialism, as it did in Nigeria. Its absence in Tanzania produced an opposite outcome. Another specific is a white settler presence, which could delay decolonisation and make it more violent, as it did in Kenya and Rhodesia.

6 The End of the British Empire

> **KEY ISSUES** What made Cyprus such a difficult decolonisation compared with the West Indies? Why did Britain withdraw from East of Suez from the late 1960s?

a) The West Indies

Decolonisation in the West Indies proved far less problematic than in either Africa or Asia. The West Indian colonies had been neglected during the inter-war depression. Early nationalist stirrings caused the Moyne Commission (1938) to recommend an extension of the franchise. Jamaica received a new constitution based upon universal suffrage in 1944. After the war Britain initiated The Federation of the West Indies (1958) to create a stronger trading partner. But it was weakly supported. Honduras and Guyana refused to join at all, and the two strongest members, Jamaica and Trinidad, left in 1962, causing it to break up. Britain granted them independence as separate nation states. Barbados followed in 1966.

Before and after independence, the Caribbean states tended to maintain close links with Britain and the United States. There have been exceptions. In Grenada, the United States made a Cold War

intervention in 1983 to overthrow a Marxist government led by
Maurice Bishop. Britain's lack of involvement illustrated how far
Caribbean affairs had passed from its hands. In Guyana, not an island
and never a part of the Federation, the Marxist influenced People's
Progressive Party was hostile to the West. Jamaica under Michael
Manley in the 1970s pursued socialist policies that extended state
influence in the bauxite mines, spent heavily on social welfare and
had good relations with Cuba.

b) Cyprus

In 1945, both Greece and Turkey laid claim to the Mediterranean
island of Cyprus. The population of the island is predominantly
Greek, with a Turkish minority. Archbishop Makarios III, the Greek
Orthodox primate of Cyprus, assumed the leadership of the *enosis*
(union with Greece) movement. Britain resisted him, despite the fact
that he was strongly anti-communist, because it did not want to offend
its ally, Turkey.

Enosis developed a terrorist wing called EOKA, led by Colonel
George Grivas, a man who had links with both monarchism and fascism in Greece. Makarios officially disassociated himself from EOKA's
indiscriminate bombings and killings. In private, however, he was in
contact with Grivas. The British exiled Makarios but, as civil war
threatened, they were forced to negotiate with him. Britain wanted to
retain Cyprus as a NATO base in the Mediterranean. Neither the
Greek nor the Turkish governments sought a resolution by violence.
All parties reached agreement in 1959 on an independent government to be led by Makarios, but with guaranteed rights for Turkish
Cypriots. Britain retained two military bases.

Independence in August 1960 did not bring peace. Civil conflict
broke out again in 1963 causing UNO intervention. A coup against
Makarios in 1974 by pro-*enosis* elements in the armed forces caused a
Turkish invasion of the North and the proclamation of a separate
state there in 1983. The problem has passed out of British hands and
into those of the UNO and the European Union. Their preferred
option of a reunited island remains unfulfilled in 2000.

Cyprus proved an intractable problem for British decolonisation.
As a European territory of strategic importance, Britain showed a
greater military commitment than in Asia, Africa or the Caribbean.
Communism was held at bay after 1945, but ethnic harmony and political stability proved elusive. Beneath these tensions lay the religious
ones between a majority Greek Orthodox and a minority Muslim
community.

c) East of Suez

Withdrawal from Aden, Yemen, Malaya and Singapore had two main origins. The first was the post-Suez waning of British will to police the region. The second was the Labour Government's dire economic problems caused by sterling crises and the 1967 devaluation of the pound. Drastic cuts in defence expenditure were necessary to pay back loans from the International Monetary Fund. The Conservatives completed withdrawal in the early 1970s.

Hong Kong remained the last important colony in Asia. In July 1997 it was returned to China after Britain's hundred-year lease expired. By the Anglo-Chinese Agreement of 1984, China gave guarantees that Hong Kong's private enterprise system would be preserved, which matched the direction its own economy was travelling in. The last Governor, Chris Patten, was less successful in protecting Hong Kong's political system from communist domination. In attempting this, he was on weak ground because British rule had never assembled a legislature elected on a full, democratic franchise.

7 Legacies of Decolonisation

> **KEY ISSUE** How has decolonisation changed the Commonwealth and Britain?

a) Expansion of the Commonwealth

Britain and the white Dominions were the original Commonwealth members of 1926. Decolonisation has turned it into a multi-racial organisation open even to states that were never in the British Empire, such as Mozambique. Not all accept the Monarch as Head of State. Many followed India in combining a Republic with continued membership. Expanding membership saw the Commonwealth, itself, become a force for further decolonisation, especially after the formation of the Organisation for African Unity (1963) which was pledged to end colonialism. The Commonwealth Prime Ministers' Conference continues to be an influential troubleshooting forum. Britain's commitment to the Commonwealth as a trading bloc has decreased since membership of the European Economic Community in 1973.

b) Post-colonial Britain

Since 1945, Britain has become a multi-cultural society, primarily due to immigration from the Commonwealth. The British Nationality Act of 1948 confirmed the right of all Commonwealth citizens to enter and become British citizens. The arrival of 492 West Indian immigrants on board the *Empire Windrush* that year proved an historic event. Initially, many of them helped fill the labour shortages in occupations such as transport and the new National Health Service. In subsequent decades, immigrants have also made such a visible contribution to multi-cultural Britain that some commentators have used the term 'reverse colonisation' to describe it. But the presence of Indian and Chinese restaurants in most high streets should not cloud the fact that upward social mobility for black and Asian Britons has been limited. They remain under-represented in most professions.

The persistence of racism in British society is a main cause of this. Legislation against discrimination has not solved the problem. The persistence of high unemployment, poor housing and police harassment has been described as 'internal colonisation,' comparing it with the formal colonisation of the past. It has contributed towards periodic riots, first in 1958 then again in 1985. The Macpherson Commission still found 'institutionalised racism' in the police force in 1999 and the Home Office has admitted to it. Since 1962, electoral opinion has been the main force behind legislation restricting immigration on grounds of colour. Margaret Thatcher frankly expressed this in claiming that white Britons feared being 'swamped' by immigrants. But no British government since 1945 has taken up the call for repatriation made by politicians like Enoch Powell. Racist parties in Britain have not had the impact of the National Front in France.

8 Conclusions

At the beginning of the chapter we asked what were the main causes of British decolonisation and how easy is it for historians to generalise. The answer is twofold. Britain shared common causes of decolonisation such as war, decline, nationalism, international relations and Cold War with other powers. Beyond that, however, it is difficult to generalise because, as a vast and complex empire, there are so many specifics that come into play. How they interacted determined the timing, protractedness, and peacefulness of each decolonisation. So, let us concentrate finally on what was specific about British decolonisation.

The British Empire emerged from the Second World War unevenly balanced and diverse. Britain itself was weaker, the Asian colonies were more advanced than the African. India was ready for independence, whereas in Africa nationalism was in no position to challenge British rule. Thus, decolonisation was spread over a long period.

It is unsurprising that Britain's response to this post-war situation was not uniform. A Labour Government was not prepared to fight to keep India, so independence came rapidly. But in Malaya later, Conservative governments used force to ensure an acceptable decolonisation that kept communism out. In Africa, the 'new imperialism' was abandoned after Suez shattered any remaining illusions about world imperial status. It was just as well that the focus of the affluent British economy in the 1950s was turning towards Europe. One year after Suez, Ghana launched an avalanche of emulatory decolonisation. Moves towards self-government were also under way in its French colonial neighbours by this time. Conservative governments came to accept the inevitability of decolonisation. Still, they did not cut and run, as the Belgians did. Representative institutions were built during the 1950s, as they had been in India before, in a preparation for self-government that contrasts with the French.

The later the decolonisation, the less control Britain had over its outcome in terms of Cold War priorities. Such was the influence of the USSR and China by the 1960s that Britain could not prevent Ghana or Tanzania from adopting socialist systems. Neither could it resist ZANU-PF in Zimbabwe. The root cause of the violence in Zimbabwe, however, was not Cold War's capacity to delay decolonisation but a white settler presence. This was also true to a degree in Kenya where the other main cause of violence was tribalism. In Nigeria tribalism was the main cause but there the violence erupted after decolonisation, not before.

References

1 John Darwin, *Britain and Decolonisation: The Retreat from Empire in the Post-War World* (Macmillan 1988), p.40.
2 Quoted in Grimal, *Decolonization*, p.115.
3 Quoted in Eric Estorick, *Stafford Cripps* (Heinemann, 1949), p.308.
4 Judith M. Brown, *Gandhi: Prisoner of Hope* (Yale University Press, 1989), p.336.
5 J.D. Hargreaves, *Decolonization in Africa* (Longman, 1988), p.109.
6 Quoted in Cain and Hopkins, *British Imperialism*, p.277.
7 Cain and Hopkins, *British Imperialism*, p.196.
8 M.E. Chamberlain, *Decolonization: The Fall of the European Empires* (Blackwell, 1985), p.50.
9 Darwin, *Britain and Decolonisation*, p.227
10 Quoted in Kevin Shillington, *Causes and Consequences of Independence in Africa* (Evans, 1997), p.45.
11 Quoted in Anthony Low, 'The End of the British Empire In Africa', in Prosser Gifford and Wm. Roger Louis (eds.), *Decolonization and African Independence: The Transfers of Power, 1960–1980* (Yale University Press, 1988), pp.53–4.
12 Quoted in Hargreaves, *Decolonization in Africa*, p.120.
13 Darwin, *Britain and Decolonisation*, p.187.
14 Hargreaves, *Decolonization in Africa*, p.131.
15 Hargreaves, *Decolonization in Africa*, p.186
16 Bethwell A. Ogot and Tiyambe Zeleza, 'Kenya: the Road to Independence and After', in Gifford and Louis, *Decolonization and African Independence*, p.426.
17 Ben Pimlott, *Harold Wilson*, HarperCollins 1992, p.369.
18 Darwin, *Britain and Decolonisation*, p.246.

Summary Diagram
British Decolonisation

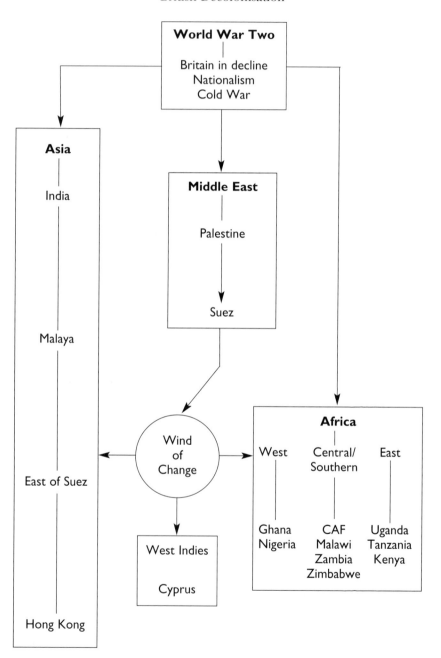

Answering source-based questions on Chapter 3

1 Gandhi and India

Read the two Gandhi extracts on page 39, and answer the following questions.

a) How would you describe Gandhi's reaction to the failure of negotiations? (*3 marks*)
b) What was the difference between Cripps' offer and what Gandhi had come to believe was necessary? (*4 marks*)
c) Why might Gandhi expect 'something more substantial' from Sir Stafford Cripps? (*5 marks*)
d) How wide a range of views about what should happen to India in 1941 are represented in these documents? (*8 marks*)

Hints and Advice

a) You need to distinguish between Gandhi's immediate reaction and the effect that failure had upon his planning for the future.
b) Here you will need to read up carefully on what Gandhi means by phrases such as 'so many limitations,' and 'the very principle of self-determination was fettered,' and compare them with what he says Britain must do in the second document.
c) Ask yourself what were the politics of the British Party that sent Cripps and if there are any similarities between them and Gandhi's own views?
d) Firstly, try to find different opinions about India from the section in which the documents are located. More specifically, ask what were the differences between Indians and Britons? Did any other nationalities have a direct interest? Finally, were there any differences between Indians or between Britons?

2 Suez Cartoons

Study the cartoons on page 49 carefully and answer the following questions:

a) Say whether the *Daily Express* supported the invasion of Suez by using the images in the cartoon. (*5 marks*)
b) Describe the Russian view of Suez using the images in the cartoon as evidence. (*5 marks*)
c) How accurate and reliable are these cartoons as sources for the history of the Suez crisis? (*10 marks*)

Hints and Advice

First, some general advice on analysing visual sources as this is the first set you have dealt with. Visual sources present us with images that we are meant to translate into words to understand their message. They have a maker (of the message) whose purpose needs to be understood. They are intended for an audience. Ask what it is, and what interpretation the maker intends them to have. Examine the details of the images for meaning. How are people, animals, or inanimate objects portrayed? Size, looks, dress, actions, landscape, architecture are all relevant.

For a), you need to identify as many of the people whose messages are stuck on Eden as possible. What view of Suez did they take and why did they take it? For b), think of which countries the sphinx, lion and cockerel represent. What is their relationship to each other in space and mood? Compare your findings with the Russian position on Suez. For c), worth double marks, draw upon your wider knowledge of what happened over Suez, compare it with the opinions of the cartoonists, and make judgements about differences and similarities, what is included and omitted. Remember cartoons usually have a propagandist content and communicate meaning through distortion and exaggeration.

Answering structured and essay questions on Chapter 3

1. Structured question
a) Identify the main areas of British decolonisation after 1945. (*3 marks*)
b) What were the principal causes of British decolonisation? (*7 marks*)
c) Assess their relative importance. (*10 marks*)

2. Essay question
Why was British decolonisation in Africa so rapid?

Hints and Advice

1. Only a few marks are available for a) so content yourself with identifying continents and sub-regions, giving clearly named examples. For b), use the suggested causes of decolonisation outlined in the introduction, then returned to in section 8, conclusions, to do the 'identifying'. For c), select some important examples of decolonisation and discuss the extent to which the causes of their decolonisation were similar or different. This 'assessment' should lead you to certain conclusions. Were there general causes common to all, but also differences in specific circumstances that affected the timing of decolonisation, whether it was peaceful or violent, and the chances of post-colonial prosperity? Answers that seek a balanced weighting of the different causes from within a broad range are likely to please the examiners.

2. You might want to question whether it was *so* rapid by including some longer-term causes. However, the 'wind of change' did blow very swiftly through Africa, so look for the reasons for this in any turning-points in British governmental attitudes, as well as pressures upon Britain from both the international context and from within the empire amongst the colonised peoples themselves.

4 French Decolonisation 1939–1962

POINTS TO CONSIDER

This chapter begins by examining how the Second World War led to the French recolonising the empire they had lost during it. It goes on to explain how this resulted in colonial wars in Indo-China and Algeria, which are contrasted with the more peaceful decolonisation achieved in sub-Saharan Africa. Finally, it summarises these developments and considers their effects upon post-colonial France.

KEY DATES

1940 Fall of France
1942 Collapse of Vichy in North Africa
1944 Brazzaville Conference
1945 Democratic Republic of Vietnam
1946 French Union
1954 Geneva Conference and Dien Bien Phu; outbreak of hostilities in Algeria
1960 Independence for most of sub-Saharan Africa
1962 Algerian independence

1 The Effects of the Second World War

> **KEY ISSUES** What effects did the war have upon the French Empire? For what reasons did the French try to re-establish colonialism after the war and with what consequences?

a) Visions in Defeat

As the Germans entered Paris in the summer of 1940, the French nation stood defeated. With defeat ended the Third Republic which, since its inception in 1870, had added much to the French Empire. Several ministers had fled to Casablanca, in Morocco, after the German invasion, from where they declared a government in exile. General Charles de Gaulle was not one of them. He had gone to London, but took heart from the fact that the empire remained undefeated. Looking back in his *Memoirs*, in 1954, he wrote:

> In the vast spaces of Africa, France could in fact rebuild its armies and reacquire its sovereignty, while awaiting the alignment of new allies along with the old to change the military balance.[1]

De Gaulle had a vision of France being regenerated through defence of the empire, like a phoenix rising from the ashes. By the end of 1940, that dream seemed to lie in tatters. His Free French Forces had failed to take back the French West African Federation, despite British naval support. The Vichy Regime (French government collaborating with the Nazis) retained control of the North and West African territories, as well as Indo-China. The Free French were isolated to Equatorial Africa and New Caledonia in the Pacific.

b) French Africa's War

Vichy rule in Africa replaced local colonial administrations with direct rule. This enabled Prime Minister Laval to carry out his deal with Hitler, to support Germany from the colonies in return for restraining Italy's ambitions to expand out of Libya. The agreement enabled Germany to threaten allied shipping off the coast of West Africa and in the Mediterranean. Consequently, the Allies decided to clear the threat by invading North Africa in November 1942. The Vichy regimes in Morocco and Algeria put up less resistance than the Germans in Tunisia, who held out until February 1942. De Gaulle's Free French forces seized the opportunity of Vichy's collapse in North Africa to take Madagascar and Réunion in the Indian Ocean, then Somaliland on the mainland of East Africa. However, the Allies remained suspicious of de Gaulle's ambitions. They saw him as a loose cannon who would put the interests of France above allied war aims. Not until 1944 did they accept his National Committee of Liberation in Algiers as a French government in waiting.

How did the war affect the development of nationalism in North Africa? It must be remembered that Africans passed from being governed by the colonial administration in 1940, to Vichy 1940–2, the Allied administration 1942–44, and the National Committee of Liberation 1944–5. It is hardly surprising that the colonial peoples were forced to make compromises. The French were prone to punish on suspicion of disloyalty. So, the Bey of Tunisia was not restored during the last years of war, the leaders of the Moroccan Independence Party were imprisoned, and the moderate, nationalist movement in Algeria, united by Ferhat Abbas in 1943, dissolved in 1945. The effect was to store up nationalism for after the war.

In sub-Saharan Africa, Vichy controlled the West while Equatorial Africa preferred de Gaulle. War stimulated economic development as raw materials and agriculture came under greater demand. The urgent need for labour mobility meant that many French Africans became free labourers for the first time, as they migrated to the growing urban areas. An urban middle-class, nationalist leadership emerged, challenging the colonialist ideology that Africans must remain assimilated with France. Leopold Senghor of Senegal was a typical voice. A lawyer, he indicted colonialism for retarding black political development. Assimilation, he declared, meant in real terms

forced labour for the African. Yet, typical of the moderate nationalism
of sub-Saharan Africa, he stopped short of demanding independence.
Instead, he recommended an imperial federation with France that
would allow colonial peoples to freely elect their representatives.

c) Brazzaville

From 1942, de Gaulle was able to embark upon the process of
imperial reconstruction he regarded as vital to restoring France as a
world power. He was anxious to head-off American attempts to prevent such recolonisation. To this end, he called a Conference of
invited colonial administrators (not elected representatives) in
Brazzaville in the French Congo, in 1944. Betts thinks that 'it now
stands as a major event in historical interpretations of decolonisation'
because it was called 'to adjust the French empire to a new world
forged during the war'.[2] But, it was only a pragmatic adjustment,
designed to try to save as much of the old colonialism as possible. On
the one hand, de Gaulle promised a new 'French Community' that
would abolish the worst aspects of colonialism, such as the legal code
that permitted forced labour. On the other, de Gaulle opposed any
move towards self-government, although he did concede local assemblies. A senior official of the US State Department criticised French
narrow mindedness:

1 There was no compromise with the basic principle that French Africa
   belongs solely to France and is an exclusively French affair. There was
   no recognition that France owed any accountability to the international
   community in the conduct of her colonial affairs and that the inter-
5 national community had any interest in such affairs.[3]

d) Indo-China: war and revolution

In Indo-China, the Japanese took advantage of French defeat in 1940.
The colonial Vichy regime, under Admiral Decoux, signed a compromise agreement by which the Japanese were allowed into the northern areas. In return, the Japanese allowed Vichy to continue to govern
until March 1945, when they launched a full-scale invasion to support
their failing war campaign in the Far East. They installed the Emperor
Bao Dai as a puppet ruler, but he was overthrown by the nationalist
coalition of the Vietminh in August, as the Japanese lost their grip.
Grimal notes the importance of the Vietminh's broad support:

> It should be pointed out that this 'August revolution' was not socialist
> in character; it was a national liberation movement in which patriots
> and democrats of all shades, Communists, nationalists ... Buddhists and
> Catholics participated in one united front.[4]

The 'August revolution' declared the Democratic Republic of
Vietnam. The French refused to recognise it, and from October 1945

the longest war of decolonisation of the twentieth century began. Vietnam was not united as a fully independent state until 1975. The colonial war against the French was a prelude to that against the world's strongest power, the United States. There is no better example of the continuity between decolonisation and Cold War conflicts.

2 The French Union (1946)

> **KEY ISSUE** What was the purpose of the French Union?

The new constitution of the Fourth Republic (1946) renamed the Empire as the French Union. There were two levels of membership. Full members like France itself, Algeria, and West and Equatorial Africa had equal citizenship. But they had only limited representation in the French Parliament. Otherwise, white Frenchmen would have become a minority in the National Assembly, and 'France would become the colony of its former colonies',[5] as a Mayor of Lyons put it. Associated states, such as Morocco, Tunis and Indo-China received internal autonomy, yet their economic and foreign policy continued to be controlled by France. As more recent additions to empire, they enjoyed only second-class status.

The French Union was based upon the principles of the Brazzaville Conference, which agreed greater autonomy for the colonial peoples and some representation in Paris. It was a concession to pressures from both the colonies themselves and the United States. Still, it amounted to considerably less than decolonisation. This was seen as unnecessary by colonial administrators like Robert Delavignette who looked to reintegration of empire by another name not dissolution.

1 … There are no longer any colonies in the old sense of the word. The colonial empire is no longer viewed in relation to the metropolis or as something different from the metropolis. The French Union is a world organization embracing both what was colonial or imperial overseas
5 and what in Europe was metropolitan. The Brazzaville Conference and the proclamation of the French Union have established the principle – and raised the problem – of a French Union superior to the old concept of colonies, empire and metropolis … The former concept of metropolis and the old concept of colony are things of the past. A new
10 idea is emerging, that of an organization shared by all but superior to each of its constituent elements. Brazzaville did not supplant Paris; Brazzaville is not the equal of Paris, but both Brazzaville and Paris belong to a new organic unit … In considering the idea of a French Union nothing could be more false or pernicious than to have at the
15 back of one's mind any idea of domination over the peoples of our overseas territories, over those we call 'natives' as opposed to 'colonials'. Tomorrow we shall all be natives of the same French Union.[6]

It is doubtful whether Africans believed this sort of propaganda any more than did the Indo-Chinese.

3 Indo-China

> **KEY ISSUES** Why did the French attempt to recolonise Indo-China? Why were they unsuccessful? How was the outcome influenced by the Cold War?

a) Recolonisation 1945–6

The new Democratic Republic of Vietnam fell immediately under threat in September 1945. The United States, despite supporting the Vietminh's wartime struggle against the Japanese, decided not to oppose French recolonisation. This decision left the Republic exposed as forces of the British Empire invaded the south in September. They paved the way for a French force of some 30,000 who took possession of Cochin-China by early 1946. Ho Chi Minh, President of the DRV, felt compelled to negotiate because he was uncertain of support from his Chinese neighbours to the north. That is why he accepted the status of a free state for Vietnam within an Indo-Chinese Federation (also consisting of Cochin-China, Laos and Cambodia) in March 1946. The Vietminh hoped to progress towards independence, particularly as the French agreed to allow Cochin-China a referendum on whether to join with Vietnam. However, the French High Commissioner, Admiral d'Argenlieu, forestalled this by declaring Cochin-China a separate republic, without even obtaining authorisation from Paris. Ho Chi Minh met the French at Fontainebleu, but the talks collapsed. Ho's insistence on eventual independence was one reason. Another was that the French Government contained sympathisers with the French settlers. They lobbied hard to protect their interests by keeping Vietnam within the French Union.

A broader explanation of the breakdown is that France's desire to reassert its imperial status converged with Cold War priorities. Communist domination of the Vietminh ensured Indo-China would become an early Cold War 'hot-spot'. This explains why the United States preferred French recolonisation to Vietnamese independence. The French wanted to restrict the Vietminh to Tonkin by building an anti-communist coalition around it. To this end, both the Cambodian and Laotian monarchies were restored. Cochin-China, economically important as the main grain-growing province, was to be used as an anti-communist power base. The Indo-Chinese Federation would keep the region politically divided and firmly under French control.

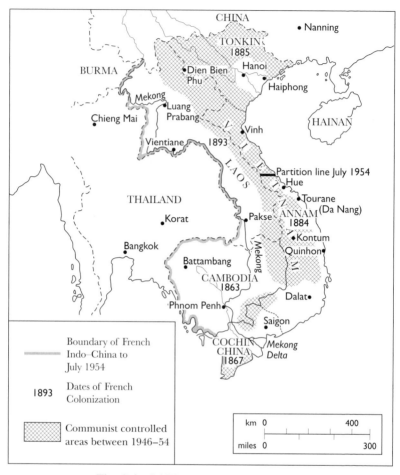

The Colonial War in Indo China, 1946–54

In trying to isolate the Vietminh, the French reckoned without the degree of popular support it had built up during the war. By not pursuing a strict communist policy of land expropriation it had even retained the support of landlords. In the towns, it was well supported by the middle class, to whose nationalist sentiments it appealed. Colonialists like d'Argenlieu were completely out of touch in believing that they could show the Vietminh how weak they were.

The French attack upon Haiphong in November 1946 killed 6,000 Vietnamese but settled nothing. It merely drove the Vietminh into underground, guerrilla warfare that lasted until 1954. From their bases in the Northern Highlands, the Vietminh harassed the French beyond their heartlands, well into Cochin-China.

HO CHI MINH (1890–1969)

Ho was born in Annam in 1890, the son of a government official who had resigned in protest against French domination of his country. He studied politics in Paris where he went on to help found the French Communist Party. From there he trained in Moscow where he was encouraged to form a broad, nationalist alliance with the bourgeoisie to overthrow imperialism. By 1925 he was in China where he set up a revolutionary youth movement for Vietnamese exiles. In 1930 he led an unsuccessful military rising against the French. Fleeing to Hong Kong, he was imprisoned by the British until 1933. On release, he returned to the USSR and then to China by 1938. In his absence, the Vietnamese Communist Party established itself amongst the peasantry of the North. It was Japanese invasion in 1940 that provided the conditions for his return to Vietnam, where he founded the Vietminh. In 1945 he became the first President of the Democratic Republic of Vietnam, the political brain behind the colonial war against the French that lasted until 1954.

As his health declined through the 1960s, he was less of an influence during the war against the South and its ally the USA. He gave up the leadership of the Party but remained important behind the scenes. Never a cult figure like Mao or Stalin, North Vietnamese knew him simply as 'Uncle Ho'. He never deviated from his conviction that Vietnam should be reunited. As the USA attacked the North in 1966 he said 'nothing is as dear to the heart of the Vietnamese as independence and liberation'. He did not live to see Vietnam unified. He died in 1969 with war against the South and its American ally still raging. But Saigon was renamed Ho Chi Minh City in 1975 to honour his contribution of leading Vietnam's struggle for decolonisation and national self-determination through communist revolution.

b) The 'Bao Dai Solution'

Bao Dai had been the Emperor of Vietnam until expelled by the Vietminh in 1945. He spent the years 1945–49 in Hong Kong. The French wrongly assumed that he could be restored as a puppet and popular figurehead to combat the Vietminh's appeal. Bao Dai's history of collaboration with both the French and Japanese made this seem optimistic. Nevertheless, by the Along Bay agreement of 1947, both parties agreed to try. Bao Dai, however, was not prepared to be quite the puppet that the French wanted. They had to accept eventual independence for Vietnam, if Bao Dai was to act as their instrument against communism. In 1948, Vietnam under Bao Dai was accepted as a state within the French Union. The next year, the independence of Vietnam under his leadership was recognised by the French Government, but no vote of the people of the newly independent state was taken.

This proved no solution to the war against the Vietminh. However, it did provide the French with a pretence for remaining in Indo-China. Bao Dai's regime was presented as an independent state under attack from communism. Once China installed a communist regime (1949), the domino theory was advanced as a justification for staying. If Indo-China fell to communism too, then who would be next? A war that had begun in 1946 over French imperialism had, in three years, mushroomed into part of a regional struggle against communism in South East Asia. Pre-war conflicts over imperialism were being subsumed into the Cold War. The United States backed the French to the hilt because they assumed that the Vietminh and even the Chinese communists were puppets of the USSR. The outbreak of the Korean War in 1950 merely confirmed them in this incorrect view.

c) 'Hell in a very small place': the road to Dien Bien Phu, 1950–54

It is probable that no single, individual influenced the outcome of the wars in Indo-China more than General Vo Nguyen Giap. Giap had obtained a doctorate in law from Hanoi University before his membership of the Indo-Chinese Communist Party drove him into exile in China during the Second World War. Returning to Vietnam in 1945, a close confidante of his fellow exile Ho Chi Minh, he led the final attack upon Hanoi that defeated the Japanese.

In the fighting against the French between 1946 and 1949, Giap masterminded the guerrilla tactics that frustrated the French. Well armed by the Chinese from 1950, however, he switched to a modern war of movement. The French had not expected the Vietminh to confront them in mass battle formation, let alone defeat them, as they did at Caobang in October 1950. The French were forced to 'Vietnamise' their armed forces by raising an army from Bao Dai's supporters. The war also became 'Americanised' in that the USA supplied $2,900 million of aid in 1950–54, and in the last year were bearing 80 per cent of the cost. By that time it was evident that, despite French hopes, the United States was not going to send troops. This was one reason why the French delayed making a major attack upon Vietminh strongholds in the north. Another was lack of support for the Bao Dai regime in the south.

In early 1954 a large army of 12,000 troops under the French General Henri Navarre got themselves surrounded in the long valley of Dien Bien Phu, in the north of Tonkin province. As Giap began his attack in March, a conference on South East Asian affairs was already sitting at Geneva, clearing up the aftermath of the Korean War. His strategy was to place maximum pressure upon the conference by winning complete military victory over the French. For almost two months the Vietminh bombarded with heavy artillery a French army unable to be relieved because its airstrips had been cut off. President Eisenhower was prepared to respond to French appeals to send in B-29 bombers from the Philippines bases, but Congress refused support. Consequently, 2,000 French died, and 10,000 were captured in what Bernard Fall has darkly called 'hell in a very small place'.[7] Ho was brighter: 'The victory is a resounding one, but it is only the beginning.'[8] It was, in fact, the beginning of the end of the first stage of Vietnam's war for independence, and it was concluded at the Geneva Conference.

d) The Geneva Conference (1954)

The Geneva agreement decolonised Vietnam into two separate states either side of the 17th parallel. Laos and Cambodia also became independent states. Therefore, it was not a permanent settlement, for the new government of North Vietnam regarded the South as still under imperialist domination. French masters had merely been exchanged for American ones. The United States never signed the settlement but agreed to abide by it. The promise of free elections for the whole of Vietnam by 1956 was not honoured because Secretary of State John Foster Dulles feared the Vietminh would win them. Instead, Bao Dai headed a compliant government in the South with Ngo Dinh Diem as Prime Minister.

So why did the North Vietnamese accept it, at least for the short-term? Firstly, the promise of French withdrawal from the region was a strong incentive. Public opinion was against the war and they left by 1956. Secondly, they were hemmed in by Cold War pressures. Dulles took a hawkish line throughout and it was not inconceivable that the USA might implement his nuclear threats. Britain wished to avoid this at all costs. North Vietnam's allies, China and the USSR, both had their reasons for wanting a settlement. China had recently been dragged into the Korean War and was not anxious to be similarly committed by her Vietnamese neighbour. Soviet priority was to get the French out of South East Asia where circumstances encouraged her to be too close an ally of the USA.

e) Assessment

Decolonisation in Indo-China, as in Burma and Indonesia, was opened up by the Japanese wartime invasion. The Vietminh became so empowered that recolonisation by the former colonial power proved impossible. In Indo-China, the historical continuity between decolonisation and the Cold War is seen at its strongest. Once it became clear that recolonisation could not prevail, the French ended up fighting a Cold War conflict. France's decline as a world power was fully exposed as she moved from imperialist to surrogate of the USA in a few years. Behind this was the equally strong link between nationalism and communism in the decolonising world. Where communism was strong within a nationalist movement, wars of decolonisation were more likely to turn into Cold War conflicts, and be prolonged. Although French decolonisation of Indo-China was complete by 1956, the Americans remained in conflict with the North Vietnamese until 1973. Not until 1975 was the spirit of Geneva, that there should be a united Vietnam, finally realised.

4 Sub-Saharan Africa

> **KEY ISSUE** Why was the decolonisation of Sub-Saharan Africa so peaceful compared with that of Indo-China?

a) The post-war background

Sub-Saharan Africa's decolonisation contrasts sharply with that of Indo-China. It is a comparative history of war and peace. The roots of difference lie in the under-development of sub-Saharan Africa. The arid landscape was virtually worthless, and the few French who lived there presided over a minimal administration. Only Senegal had any representation in the French parliament though it did have the distinction of sending the first black African there: Blaise Diagne in 1912. The French paid little attention to education. A small elite was trained up for the civil service where they took the best jobs and remained loyal.

We have already seen how de Gaulle's Free French forces moved into sub-Saharan Africa to oppose Vichy from 1940. At the end of the war, the region was organised into two: French West Africa and French Equatorial Africa, ruled from Dakar (Senegal) and Brazzaville (Congo) respectively. The Brazzaville Conference encouraged Africans to think only of greater autonomy, not independence, confirmed by the constitutional arrangements of the French Union. Africans had slightly expanded representation in Paris but it was limited by what Hargreaves calls an 'oligarchical franchise'. The French called it a dual college system. It was complicated, but essentially it meant that white French votes counted for much more than black African ones, and that a quota system operated in Paris that prevented too many black delegates being elected.

b) French reforms 1946–56

Wartime changes had enabled some development of nationalist politics. In October 1946, the Democratic African Rally (RDA) was formed under the initiative of Félix Houphouet-Boigny, a former Ivory Coast doctor turned planter, and leader of its Democratic Party. Rivalry for regional political leadership caused Senghor in Senegal to stay out of the RDA and form his own party (IOM). In Paris, these African parties attached themselves to French ones. The RDA's links with the French Communist Party caused colonial administrations in Africa to treat it with harsh suspicion, although he later proved a moderate President of the Ivory Coast (1965–90).

In the decade after 1946, a public investment programme, known as FIDES, aimed to develop the colonies in order to rescue the war-torn national economy. It brought about improvements in agriculture and transport. Social services, such as education and health care, were expanded, creating jobs in the bureaucracy for Africans. The first significant examples of private investment also took place. As urbanisation accelerated, impoverished rural migrants flocked into the towns. But the investment favoured the already more developed coastal regions at the expense of the interior. There, the French appealed to the enterprise of the privileged elites.

c) The loi-cadre (1957)

The outline law (*loi-cadre*) of 1957 placed the African colonies on a new constitutional footing. Like FIDES it was recognition that colonialism could not survive unreformed. It broke up the two federations of French West Africa and French Equatorial Africa. Each colony was now to have a separate relationship with the centre (Paris). Critics like Senghor accused France of defending colonialism by divide and rule tactics. He thought its result would be 'the Balkanisation of Africa'. Yet, it was a recognition that the French Union of 1946 had not gone far enough in devolving power to the colonies. Territorial Assemblies were to be elected by universal suffrage and were to enjoy increased powers devolved from Paris. The dual college system, that had disadvantaged Africans, was abolished. Nevertheless, the *loi-cadre* was intended only to advance self-government, not independence.

The *loi-cadre* caused a crisis amongst the African parties. Advanced territories like the Ivory Coast were happy to go it alone as states-in-waiting, but the poorer members, whose views were voiced by Senghor of Senegal, preferred to keep the former large federations, within which they felt protected. This raises the question of why the French were pushing reforms that most Africans did not seem ready for. The answer lies in pressures emanating from the escalating crisis in Algeria. The thinking in Paris was that one colonial war was quite enough; in sub-Saharan Africa early reform would forestall another crisis. Ironically, the *loi-cadre* generated demands for independence hardly present before. The other cause of these was the independence of neighbouring Ghana in 1957.

d) From French Community to Independence, 1958–60

The Constitution of the new Fifth Republic (1958), brought about by the Algerian crisis, brought independence a step nearer for sub-Saharan Africa. President de Gaulle asked all the colonies to vote in a referendum on whether they wanted to retain their connection with France. They could join a French Community within which France would retain control of their foreign and defence policies. All except Guinea voted yes, reflecting the nervousness that still existed about independence. French aid to Guinea was promptly withdrawn. De Gaulle's revenge stripped it of everything, down to its French-supplied telephones! Yet, this failed to sabotage Guinea as a state for the Russians knew how to install telephone lines too. All de Gaulle's petulance achieved was the loss of Sekou Toure's new state to the communist bloc. More conservative states like Ivory Coast were anxious that, even if independence were thrust upon them, a strong economic link should be maintained. Without it, Houphouet-Boigny predicted, lay only poverty and anarchy. Membership of the French Community simply dissolved through 1960 as one by one its members left, reassured that France would not do what it had done to Guinea. The French Community had hardly existed as a constitutional form, except as a transitional bridge to independence.

So the pattern by which sub-Saharan Africa achieved its independence contrasted starkly with that of Indo-China and Algeria. The peaceful devolution of sovereignty was an important propagandist coup for a French government that was simultaneously embroiled in a vicious colonial war elsewhere. It enabled the violent decolonisation of Algeria to be presented as a special case. In sub-Saharan Africa, decolonisation had arrived rapidly. In 1946 it had not been on the French agenda and sub-Saharan politics scarcely had an agenda. As late as 1958 all territories except Guinea elected to retain the colonial connection, an indication of the economic progress they had made under FIDES. In 1960, they had to be virtually pushed into independence by an exhausted colonial France. By that time the post-war investment programme in the African colonies had become a tremendous burden upon the French taxpayer. Private capital was comparatively uninterested in the colonies compared with Europe.

5 North Africa

KEY ISSUES Why did France pursue such different policies towards decolonisation in Algeria compared with Morocco and Tunisia? To what extent was colonial war in Algeria fought for similar reasons to that in Indo-China?

a) Morocco and Tunisia

Both Morocco and Tunisia achieved independence within a month of each other in 1956. They were newer colonies, had a much smaller French settler population than Algeria, and had only associated status under the 1946 Constitution. All these factors made the decolonisation of Morocco and Tunisia easier than that of Algeria.

In Morocco, the Istiqlal Party had been founded in 1944 to press for independence. It was conservative in supporting the establishment of a constitutional monarchy under the Sultan Mohamed V. The Sultan's identification with the urban Istiqlal Party alienated him from the feudal Berber lords in the rural hinterland. Deepening urban unrest led to a major confrontation between strikers and police in Casablanca in December 1952. The French response to growing nationalism in 1953 was to replace the Sultan with the compliant Mulat Arafa and his Berber supporters. This failed, as the nationalists launched a terrorist campaign, provoking a counter-organisation from the settler class called 'French Presence' (1955). When it became clear that Moroccans in the Army were prepared to intervene on the side of the nationalists, the Sultan had to be brought back to reign over an independent country, in March 1956.

In Tunisia, the Neo-Destour Party had merged into a broader Tunisian Front in 1946. Under the leadership of Habib Bourguiba it grew into a mass party of half a million members. Bourguiba, later to be the President of Tunisia for 30 years, was imprisoned regularly over two decades by the French for agitating for independence. Bourguiba's nationalist movement persuaded the French Foreign Minister, Robert Schuman, to grant self-government in 1951. This was suspended, however, on disruption by settlers collaborating with the Army, and was only restored in 1955 after the Indo-Chinese settlement. The French Government decided to leave Tunisia in order to concentrate upon the Algerian problem.

b) Algeria

i) 'The era of broken promises', 1945–54

Just as the Second World War ended, the peace in Algeria was broken by terrible violence. Here are two historians' accounts of the events in Sétif, in May 1945, that set Algeria on a path of colonial war. The first is from Raymond Betts:

1 there was an uprising and riot in Sétif, an essentially Muslim town west of Constantine and beyond the mainstream of French colonial activities. On 8 May, as the French gathered together in the town square to begin their celebrations of the European peace achieved on V-E Day, a group
5 of Muslims, carrying revolutionary banners and moving angrily forward, struck out at the crowd.

What precipitated this uprising and exactly how it began are still matters of debate. However, it is certain that the mob was spurred on by
economic deprivation as well as the desire for colonial reform. During
10 the next five days, as the helpless French were assailed, the violence to
person and to property was horrible. Then French troops finally arrived
and the bloody tide swept the other way. This bidirectional frenzy
whipped up lasting anger and animosity – some consider the events at
15 Sétif the awakening of an Algerian national spirit of independence – and
left behind an appalling, if ill-determined number of dead, between 1,000
and 6,000 persons.[9]

The second account is from J.R. Hargreaves:

1 Frustrated in their claims for equality, and radicalised by wartime hard-
ships, many Algerians began to talk of independence: this was among
the slogans with which the people of Sétif, near Constantine, celebrated
Victory Day on 8 May 1945. When the police tried to seize their ban-
5 ners fighting broke out, followed by violent attacks on settler families;
over a hundred Europeans were murdered, and others robbed,
wounded or raped. There followed the bloodiest repression seen in
Africa since the colonial 'pacification'. Muslim victims were numbered in
thousands; hopes of solving Algeria's problems through Franco-Muslim
10 partnership were fatally damaged; and anti-Western feeling throughout
the Arab world received a new stimulus.[10]

It is clear that the Algerians of Sétif felt that the end of the war
brought little to celebrate. A third account, by Henri Grimal, offers
definite opinions about the causes of the violence:

1 The numerically dominant Muslim community ... increasingly rapidly,
had demonstrated against the oppression which it had suffered in the
social, intellectual, economic and political fields in relation to the French
minority who, whether French by birth or by adoption, traditionally
5 enjoyed the perks.[11]

Algeria had been a French colony since 1834. The *colons* (European
colonists) in Algeria were mostly French, although there were a few
Italians. They were known as *pieds noirs* (black feet) by Arabs because
of their fondness for wearing cheap black shoes. By 1945 they numbered about one million (10 per cent), having settled in large numbers since the mid-nineteenth century. Originally small landowners
who had dispossessed Arabs, many had migrated to the towns where
they were in direct competition with Arabs for jobs. As a province of
France, Algeria sent members to the National Assembly, but they were
elected from separate colleges, which weighted representation
against Arabs in Paris. After Sétif, a Statute of 1947 gave Algeria its
first parliament, but it continued to discriminate against Arabs in a
number of ways. Firstly, the Algerian Constituent Assembly gave equal
weight to the two communities, despite the numerical supremacy of
the Arabs. In any case, many *colons* thought that Arabs should not be

allowed to vote at all, so they gerrymandered elections. Secondly, if a contentious issue came up threatening the interests of *colons*, the Governor-General had the right to insist upon a two-thirds majority being necessary. Thirdly, the promise to allow the use of Arabic as a language of instruction was not kept.

'The era of broken promises', as he called it, disillusioned even moderates like Ferhat Abbas. Originally a supporter of Algerian autonomy within the French Union, this small-town pharmacist eventually became the leader of the revolutionary National Liberation Front (FLN). The FLN was founded by a group of exiles, including Abbas and Ben Bella, in Cairo in 1954. It emerged out of a number of smaller organisations. From its seat of government in exile in Cairo, the FLN organised its campaign for independence. Although it declared itself to be a democratic socialist organisation in aspiration, it planned to wage a terrorist and guerrilla war against the French.

ii) The Battle for Algeria, 1954–58

Although it began relatively quietly in 1954, the FLN's insurrection became so serious by 1958 that it brought down the Fourth French Republic. Supplied with arms via Morocco, the FLN launched their terrorist war proper with a full-scale attack upon the town of Philippeville in March 1955. Collaborating Arabs, as well as *colons* and French forces, were targeted in a ruthlessly determined attack. The French response was twofold. On the one hand, 400,000 extra troops were dispatched. On the other, a more liberal Governor, Jacques Soustelle, was sent to attend to economic and social reform. This came too late to affect Algeria's chronic rural poverty, caused by a technically neglected agriculture unable to support a growing population. Migrants moved to the towns, where they joined a growing educated class who could not find jobs because the *colons* monopolised them.

The Army played a crucial role in the politics of Algerian decolonisation. It had been badly wounded by the defeat in Indo-China. Many senior officers took the view that they had been betrayed by the politicians and were determined not to let it happen again in Algeria. It formed a natural alliance with the *colons* in keeping Algeria French. Governments in Paris dithered, however, as the FLN's pressure mounted. Guy Mollet's Socialist administration said it would negotiate with the rebels, but only once the violence had ceased. Left-wing politicians, socialist or communist, were hardly more sympathetic to decolonisation than the Right. This was because they sought the votes of the working-class *pieds noirs*. Their protests forced Mollet to appoint a less liberal Governor, Robert Lacoste, in 1956 and to give him special powers to deal with the emergency.

He was to need them. From September 1956, the FLN switched strategy and began an urban guerrilla campaign targeting the capital,

Algiers. For over a year, *colons,* Arabs deemed to be collaborators, and members of the armed forces became the victims of terror. The French public became accustomed to pictures in their morning newspapers of bombed-out cafés in which women and children had died. But the Army would not yield, and there was much support in France for sending 8,000 extra paratroopers to wage *The Battle of Algiers,* as Gillo Pontecorvo's great film of 1966 called it. A counter-insurgency strategy fought terror with terror, as the French forces demonstrated to the FLN that they too could torture and kill indiscriminately. The FLN were quelled but not beaten by the end of 1957. By the end of the Algerian war one million had died and up to one third of the 9 million population displaced in the most violent of all decolonisations.

An important political shift had taken place as a result of the Battle of Algiers. The Army had asserted its autonomy over the Algerian colonial administration and Paris by taking its counter-insurgency tactics to unauthorised lengths. In February, the United Nations condemned a French air violation of Tunisian territory for the purpose of strafing a FLN village. In May 1958, the *colons* installed their own 'Committee of Public Safety' under General Massu, a *de facto* illegal government. The Army watched in approval. It was clear that Paris was no longer in control of Algeria. There was a real possibility that the Army might overthrow the Government in France by a *coup d'état.* The Pflimlin administration that was in power in May 1958 contained no supporter of keeping Algeria French. The civilian and military powers were in direct opposition. It was this crisis that persuaded the National Assembly to effectively vote the Fourth Republic out of existence. They invited Charles de Gaulle, who had held no political office since his resignation from the Presidency in January 1946, to become Prime Minister. Peter Neville nicely captures the farce that French politics had been reduced to.

1 The government in Paris was in a state of panic, while the rebel army
    generals appealed to de Gaulle to save 'French Algeria'. As the republi-
    can government had no idea how to solve the crisis, it was by no means
    unhappy to turn matters over to the General once more. So it was that
5 on 28 May 1958 de Gaulle got 'the call', which he had waited 12 years
    to receive.[12]

In January 1959, de Gaulle assumed office as the powerful President he had always wanted to be, after the French people had given him overwhelming approval for a new Constitution. The Fifth Republic had commenced. It was the first example in the twentieth century of decolonisation causing regime replacement in Europe. But de Gaulle was not the Army's stooge. He was seen as a compromise candidate who might bridge the gaps, and did not have overwhelming support in the Army or Parliament. As Ferro argues, Gaullism went on to capture the colonialist movement, not vice versa. Within four years Algeria was given independence.

iii) 'The day of the pigs': the end of French Algeria, 1958–62

De Gaulle employed a combination of 'hot and cold' tactics to bring Algeria back under the control of the civilian government in Paris. Firstly, he allowed General Challe to devastate the FLN bases with helicopter support for combat teams on the ground. The *colons* and the Army anticipated complete military victory, but de Gaulle's aim was to force a weakened FLN to the negotiating table. At the same time, he announced reforms in housing, education and public works schemes to appease the Arabs, and their sympathisers in France. He also reassured the oil companies that he would protect their interests in the Algerian Sahara.

Through 1959, de Gaulle was moving towards those who saw France's future in the leadership of the EEC not as a colonial power. By September, he had come around to offering the FLN a clear choice, if they halted hostilities. Firstly, they could make the unlikely choice of continuing in union with France. Secondly, de Gaulle's preference was to have a looser association by which France would continue economic and social investment in return for control of defence and foreign policy. Thirdly, they could opt for independence.

This was a watershed offer by de Gaulle because it acknowledged that, in agreed conditions, Algerians had a right to decide their own destiny. It was too much for the extremists amongst the *colons* who rioted in Algiers during the 'week of the barricades', January 1960, and shot at the police while the Army looked on. De Gaulle was forced to visit Algiers in March to reassure those who feared a sell-out to the FLN. He had limited success but sat down with the FLN anyway, in constant fear that the street demonstrations might spill over into an army *coup*. Cleverly, de Gaulle obtained support for his policies from a referendum of the French people in January 1961. This provoked the long-expected Algiers *coup* in April, which was unsuccessful because de Gaulle talked it down with a direct radio broadcast to the troops. Robert Buron, one of his ministers, called it the 'victory of the transistors.'[13] The military malcontents went underground. They formed the OAS (*Organisation Armée Secrète*), a counter-terrorist organisation that operated in both Algeria and France. No target was too big or too small for the OAS. A plan to bomb the Eiffel Tower failed, but they succeeded in maiming the four-year old child of the Minister of Culture, André Malraux. On the evening of 22 August 1962, just after 8pm, as he was on his way from Paris to the airport at Villacoublay, de Gaulle's car was fired upon. The quick-minded chauffeur, Francis Marroux, accelerated on seeing the danger and the bullets missed their target. Relief was short-lived. Two more cars appeared and pumped fourteen more bullets into de Gaulle's vehicle. Two tyres and the gearbox were damaged.

De Gaulle's biographer completes a narrative so astonishing it inspired a work of fiction by Frederick Forsyth, *The Day of the Jackal*.

1   Fortunately, in the twilight, Marroux, driving on one gear, managed to lose his pursuers, and they made the airport at Villacoublay – with difficulty, but without serious casualty. The General and Mme de Gaulle were covered in glass, but there was nothing worse than that, apart
5   from shock ...[14]

The shock had eased by the time the General telephoned his Prime Minister, Georges Pompidou, later that evening. 'They shot like pigs', he said.

The irony of this assassination attempt is that it came some seven weeks after Algerian independence. It was purely revengeful. The Evian talks that began in May 1961 had finally concluded in March 1962, and the Algerians voted for independence on 1st July. The most important aspects of the Evian agreement were as follows. Firstly, the FLN were to cease-fire in order for elections to be held. Secondly, the *colons* were given three years to decide whether they wanted to remain French or become Algerian citizens. If they opted for French citizenship, they would not enjoy full civil rights in Algeria. In practice, almost all returned to France. 85,000 pro-French Muslims (*harkis*) also went to France. Thirdly, French companies were allowed leasing rights to continue to develop oil fields, but they had no ownership of them. Fourthly, France was allowed to maintain the important naval base at Mers-el-Kebir for a minimum of fifteen years (in practice, she withdrew as early as 1968).

iv) Assessment: the nature of Algerian decolonisation

Algeria was France's last major decolonisation. After the bloody conflict in Indo-China, it exhausted her capacity to retain an empire. As in Indo-China, the French militarily resisted nationalism because they prioritised the interests of a substantial settler population that was influential in French politics. That the Algerian war began the very year the Indo-Chinese one ended, shows that the French did not think there were any 'universal lessons of decolonisation' to be learned. They reacted according to the specific, internal dynamics of the situation.

The nature of nationalism made a difference to French stubbornness in decolonising Algeria. A central argument of Frantz Fanon's best-selling *The Wretched of the Earth* (1961) was that colonialism could only be removed by violence. The FLN ruthlessly announced that the French could leave with a suitcase or in a coffin, and this provoked counter-ruthlessness. The nationalist movement also fought an internecine war, between the FLN and its rival the MNA, that killed thousands. Eventually, the costs of policing such disorder became unsustainable upon the metropole, and France sought a compromise. Ferro emphasises the leading role played by metropolitan intellectuals in swaying public opinion. McWilliams and Piotrowski argue that, 'Many French (not unlike many of their U.S. counterparts during the war in Vietnam) became more concerned about the effect the killing, the brutality, and the torture had on their own society than their impact on the Arab victims.[15] Holland sees the role of 'Eurocentric technocrats', who wanted to abandon empire to concentrate upon Western markets, as crucial. If so, then it is to be remembered that France only left once the leasehold rights on the valuable Algerian oil deposits were secured.

Finally, what role did the superpowers play in Algerian decolonisation? In the USA, both Eisenhower and Kennedy were critical of the French Army in Algeria and grew reluctant to defend it against the Third World in the United Nations. Despite the leftist politics of the FLN, they were neither communists nor aligned with the USSR. There was an Algerian Communist Party but it was discredited amongst Arab nationalists because it followed the line of its French comrades. The French CP was strong and in perpetual hope of power. Because it participated in coalition governments, it became tarred with their policies. It had a vision of Algeria as a communist province of a communist France, modelled on the Muslim republics of the USSR. Islam acted as a strong, anti-communist barrier in Algeria, and the USA was less concerned that communism would prevail there than in Indo-China.

6 Conclusions

> **KEY ISSUES** How important are the following in understanding the character of French decolonisation: war, violence, nationalism, communism, economic interests? To what extent have post-colonial Algeria, Vietnam, sub-Saharan Africa, and France itself been affected by decolonisation?

a) The nature of French decolonisation

The effects of the Second World War were more destabilising upon French colonialism than upon British. French defeat by both Germany and Japan left it in a weaker position to reclaim its empire after the war. In the case of Indo-China, this was never fully achieved, even in the short-term. In North and sub-Saharan Africa, the war had brought profound economic and social changes, such as urbanisation, that assisted the growth of nationalism.

In two out of the three main areas considered, French decolonisation was extremely violent. In Indo-China, this was because nationalism had taken power by the end of the war and proved impossible to dislodge. The fact that it was communist-led provoked a stronger counter-revolution from France supported by the United States. In addition, a strong settler class wished to hold on to valuable economic interests. In contrast to Algeria, the French left an *incomplete* decolonisation. In Algeria, nationalism also emerged from the war strengthened, but not so much as in Indo-China. The settler class defended its interests just as strongly, and obtained firm support from an Army propelled by its earlier defeat in Indo-China. Resistance to decolonisation was again motivated by valuable economic interests.

Sub-Saharan Africa was peaceful by comparison because it had less economic value, no settler class of any consequence, and its nationalism was exceptionally moderate with no trace of communism. France had no strong reasons for remaining, and actually had to initiate decolonisation, according to writers like Betts, who may underestimate the strength of nationalism.

A principal reason for willingness to withdraw from sub-Saharan Africa was to concentrate upon Algeria. This emphasises the interconnections between decolonisations. The character of one could be affected by the pattern of another. Algeria was tougher because Indo-China came before; but sub-Saharan Africa was easier because Algeria had become so violent.

b) Post-colonial consequences

Ben Bella's socialist regime in Algeria was quickly overthrown by Boumédienne in 1965. When a quarter of a century of his authoritarian socialism failed to significantly deliver the promise of decolonisation – higher living standards – Algeria became an early example of the Islamic fundamentalist revival. The Islamic Salvation Front won the 1991 elections, but military rule was imposed in 1992 and the results cancelled. Through the 1990s, Algeria was wracked by a terrorism that took a terrible revenge. Over a quarter of a million Algerians had died in the struggle against the French. In 1985, before the fundamentalist insurrection began, Robert Holland wrote that the violent nature of Algerian decolonisation bequeathed a violent legacy. This now reads like a tragic prophecy.

The war fought by the Vietnamese to rid themselves of the French merged into a renewed anti-colonial one against the Americans through the 1960s. It took until 1973 for the United States to leave and until 1975 for the civil war to end in a united Vietnam under communist rule. In the 1980s, Vietnam became involved in further wars for regional supremacy with Cambodia, Laos and China. Only through the 1990s did the state begin to fulfil some of the hopes of decolonisation by stabilising its diplomatic relations and opening up its economy to more foreign trade, most notably with the United States.

Sub-Saharan Africa has declined since decolonisation. Economically and ecologically the most deprived part of the continent, it inherited a legacy of poverty that led to political instability. At the root of poverty were climatic disadvantages and a technologically backward agriculture unable to support a growing population. This created a need to borrow, which led to a new, post-colonial, type of dependency. In a vain attempt to pay off debts farming was turned over to cash crops for export earnings. The condition of such states at the beginning of the twenty-first century provides the strongest argument behind the world movement to abolish Third World debt.

For France, the economic consequences of decolonisation have been the opposite. The turn towards Europe and free trade to replace the soaring costs of empire resulted in increased prosperity. Immigration has acted as a reminder that poverty persists in the former empire. Like its neighbour, Britain, France has turned into a multicultural nation. Unlike Britain, however, a racist political party, the National Front, has had considerable success at elections. Led by a former paratrooper in Algeria, Jean Marie Le Pen, the National Front advocates an end to all immigration, and repatriation to be encouraged by discrimination in the levels of welfare benefits. It also blames immigrants for rises in crime rates. When the French soccer team won the 1998 World Cup, Le Pen said, 'I claim this victory for the National Front, which designed its framework'.[16] It was difficult to see how, when ten of the squad members were either born outside metropolitan France or had parents who were. Ironically, one of them was France's outstanding player, Zinedine Zidane, whose parents were *harkis* (pro-French, Muslim emigrants from Algeria). Zidane's two goals in the 3–0 victory over Brazil, resulted in white, black and Arab French uniting in national celebration on 12 July 1998. But, when the party was over, many of them returned to their *quartiers difficiles* (inner suburbs), where unemployment rates of up to 50 per cent testified to one failure of decolonisation. In those difficult districts ferments what one of the finest French films of the 1990s called simply *La Haine* (The Hate).

References

1 Quoted in Raymond F. Betts, *France and Decolonisation, 1900–1960* (Macmillan, 1991), p.50.
2 Betts, *France and Decolonisation*, p.59.
3 Ralph Bunche, quoted in Betts, *France and Decolonisation*, p.61.
4 Grimal, *Decolonization*, p.236.
5 Edouard Herriot, quoted in Betts, *France and Decolonisation*, p.70.
6 R. Delavignette, in *Esprit* July 1945, quoted in Grimal, *Decolonization*, p.175.
7 Quoted in Wayne C. McWilliams and Harry Piotrowski, *The World Since 1945. A History of International Relations* (Rienner, 1997), p.120.
8 Quoted in Betts, *France and Decolonisation*, p.91.
9 Betts, *France and Decolonisation*, pp.97–8.
10 Hargreaves, *Decolonization in Africa*, p.70.
11 Grimal, *Decolonization*, p.382.
12 Peter Neville, *France 1914–69: The Three Republics* (Hodder and Stoughton, 1995), p.117.
13 Quoted in Keith Panter-Brick, 'Independence, French Style', in Gifford and Louis (ed.), *Decolonization and African Independence*, p. 99.
14 Charles Williams, *The Last Great Frenchman. A Life of General de Gaulle* (Abacus, 1993), p.406.
15 McWilliams and Piotrowski, *The World Since 1945*, p.136.
16 *The Guardian*, 14 July 1998.

Summary Diagram
French Decolonisation

	Indo-China	North Africa	Sub-Saharan Africa	Metropole (France)
Effects of Second World War	Japanese occupation 1940	Axis invasion; defeat of by 1942	Conflict between Vichy and Free French	• German occupation • colonial defeat • economic devastation
Effects of Nationalism	Vietminh established Democratic Republic of Vietnam 1945	• Setif riots (1945) in Algeria • Nationalist parties eg, Neo Destour, Istiqlal, FLN	Nationalism minimal until RDA (1946); moderate from then	Concessions • Brazzaville 1944 • French Union (1946) • *Loi cadre* 1957 • French Community (1958)
Communism and Cold War	• Ho Chi Minh Marxist educated and trained • Chinese Revolution (1949) • Korean War (1950–53)	Less important than in Indo-China; Soviet support for FLN	Never a Cold War 'hotspot'	• US support for war in Indo- China • concern over Algeria
Colonial War and Independence	• French Recolonisation (1946) • War until Geneva Conference separated N. from S. Vietnam (1954)	• Algerian war (1954–62) • Morocco and Tunisia obtained independence without war (1956)	No wars, little violence before independence in 1960	Independence resisted in Indo-China and Algeria

Source-based questions on Chapter 4

Read the accounts by Betts, Hargreaves and Grimal on pages 79–80 again, and answer the questions below.

a) What are the main similarities in the accounts by Betts and Hargreaves? (*5 marks*)
b) What are the main differences? (*5 marks*)
c) How did Algerian nationalism demonstrate against 'the oppression which it had suffered' (Grimal) in the years 1954–62? (*10 marks*)

Hints and advice

a) This should be straightforward if you look at comments on some of the causes, how the French behaved, and the significance of the riots.
b) Examine closely the emphasis each gives to the type of causes that sparked the riots. Consider the evidence of casualties. Are there any differences in the type of words used that might indicate approval or disapproval by the writer of riotous behaviour? And, how critical is each writer of the French?
c) Here, you must look beyond the riots to their consequences as a stage in the development of Algerian nationalism. 'Oppression' can be shown by giving evidence of Algerian grievances against the French. The 'demonstrate' part needs detailed information of nationalist tactics in the war and a judgement about how successful they were. Remember to give plenty of supporting evidence because this is a 10 mark question.

Essay Questions on Chapter 4

1. Compare and contrast the decolonisations in Indo-China, Algeria and sub-Saharan Africa.
2. Discuss the view that the main characteristic of French decolonisation was war.

Comparative Decolonisations: the Netherlands, Belgium and Portugal

5

KEY DATES

1945 Japanese defeat in Asia
1949 Dutch agree independence for Indonesia
1954 End of Indonesian union with Dutch
1959 Leopoldville Riots
1960 Independence of the Congo
1961 Start of colonial wars in Portuguese Africa
1974 Portuguese Revolution
1975 Independence of Angola and Mozambique

1 Introduction: Patterns of Colonisation of Three European Powers

KEY ISSUE How different were the colonial histories of the Netherlands, Portugal and Belgium?

When decolonisation began after the Second World War Portugal and the Netherlands were both old colonial empires. The dictator-ship encouraged the ten million Portuguese to see themselves as the guardians of a rich cultural inheritance, a Lusophone (Portuguese speaking) world of 150 million people spread across four continents, making it the fifth most commonly spoken language in the world. The Dutch, like the Portuguese, were old colonialists who had estab-lished a seafaring empire across the globe. By 1945 it had dwindled, but survived in a few places like the Dutch East Indies (Indonesia). The Belgians, by contrast, were late arrivals to colonialism. The nation state had been formed only in 1839, when independence from the Dutch was won. The Belgians planted themselves in the heart of the

'Scramble for Africa': the Congo. Like the British and French, each of these empires dissolved in the three decades between 1945 and 1975.

2 Dutch Decolonisation of Indonesia

> **KEY ISSUES** How did the Second World War weaken Dutch colonialism? Why did they fail to recolonise Indonesia?

a) Dutch Colonialism in the East Indies

The origins of the Dutch Empire lay in its glorious, seventeenth-century 'Golden Age' of trade expansion. Bourgeois merchants organised voyages by the Dutch East Indies Company and others who sailed to the West Indies, Brazil, India, Ceylon, West and South Africa. Like the Portuguese before them the Dutch discovered the routes that made a small nation great. Unlike the Portuguese, the pursuit of profit consumed missionary zeal completely. By the end of the seventeenth century the Dutch had amassed an 'embarrassment of riches.'[1] The merchants were religious men, Calvinists who worried that they had become too rich to be saved. But children in the Dutch East Indies knew little about this history at the turn of the twentieth century, for there were few schools.

Before the First World War, the Dutch state had given up its monopoly over rubber, palm oil, iron ore and petroleum deposits and allowed private companies to lease the land rights. Peasants had their land seized by these companies and were forced to labour cheaply and pay high taxes. Despite this, the traditional social structure of the Indonesian village changed little. The Dutch supported it by governing through protégé chiefs, a form of indirect rule similar to that used by the British in parts of Africa. But real power lay with the colonial bureaucracy. The representative councils had limited authority, although the establishment of a National Assembly (*Volksraad*) in 1916 did provide a forum for nationalist discussions.

Inter-war depression deepened discontent with colonialism. Higher taxation forced the smallholder into debt, businessmen suffered from export duties. Fewer business opportunities caused the middle class to clamour for the few available posts within the bureaucracy. A measure of the discrimination exercised against Indonesians is that in 1938 they occupied only 6.4 per cent of higher-grade posts compared to 92.2 per cent held by Europeans. The pattern was reversed in lower grade posts, where 98.9 per cent were Indonesians against 0.6 per cent for Europeans.

Another means of discrimination was language. Indonesians were discouraged from learning Dutch, which excluded all but a few from top jobs. Indeed, Indonesians were discouraged from learning. Only about 5 per cent attended any type of school before the Second

World War. But this backfired on the Dutch. In place of Dutch, Malay spread as the common language, and speaking it became a cultural statement of opposition to colonialism.

b) The Rise of Indonesian Nationalism

Nationalism developed early in Indonesia, encouraged by the language policy described above. It was also helped by the fact that Dutch colonialism had welded the many islands that made up the archipelago into a common political unit. Also, Indonesia had an elite educated in Dutch universities who returned with Western liberal and Marxist ideas. They developed a theory of exploitation that was applied to colonialism. As one nationalist put it, 'Indonesia is the milch cow of Holland.'[2] Although peasants were increasingly migrating to the towns for work, the strong village culture saw them return regularly. Thus, they acted as vehicles of nationalist ideas from the towns. Finally, Indonesian nationalism drew upon Islam to demand social justice and political equality from the Dutch.

The first Indonesian nationalist party, Sarekat Islam, was founded in 1912. After the Russian Revolution of 1917, it became more class conscious and demanded independence. By 1920, the Indonesian Communist Party (PKI) emerged out of a split from it. The PKI refused co-operation with other nationalists and launched an insurrection in 1926. Failure forced it underground. The Nationalists remained the strongest anti-colonial party but, to combat Dutch penetration, even they were forced to imitate the Communists' secrecy. From 1939, the Nationalists broadened their base into a united front, the Federation of Indonesian Political Parties (GAPI). In return for a democratic parliament, they offered the Dutch a common front against fascism, but were refused. As a result, Indonesian nationalists offered no support for the plight of the Netherlands at war, as this statement from one of its leaders makes clear.

1   The fall of Holland evoked secret satisfaction ... The consciousness of
    foreign domination coupled with an intense desire for freedom and inde-
    pendence became increasingly strong. As the war developed ... the
    people derived a vicarious satisfaction from the misfortunes of their
5   rulers ... For the average Indonesian, the war was not really a world con-
    flict between two great world forces. It was simply a struggle in which the
    Dutch colonial rulers finally would be punished by providence for the evil,
    the arrogance and the oppression they had brought to Indonesia ...[3]

Sjahrir's comments are useful evidence for the historian of the effects of war upon colonialism. They show how the experience of war can be differently interpreted by the peoples undergoing it. Whereas, the 'Dutch war' had been one of defeat and retreat in the face of fascism, the 'Indonesian war' was one of opportunity to be free of, and to take revenge upon, colonialism.

c) The Consequences of War and Japanese Occupation

The Second World War made an enormous impact upon colonialism in S.E. Asia. The reason for this was that during the war Japan occupied large parts of the sub-continent, driving out the colonial powers. Although Japan was militarily defeated in 1945, the impact of its wartime presence changed so much in the colonies that a restoration of the pre-war pattern of colonial rule proved impossible. This was the case (as we saw in Chapter 4) when the French tried to turn the clock back in Indo-China. It also happened in the Dutch Empire.

Between February and March 1942 Dutch colonialism in Indonesia collapsed before the Japanese invasion. Japanese success was not due to any great superiority in numbers, but to her enemy's under-estimation of her intentions and determination. The Japanese set about completely obliterating Dutch influence. The Dutch government, exiled in London because of the Nazi invasion, was powerless.

The Japanese lacked the manpower to annex its new empire, so they called it the Greater East Asian Co-Prosperity Sphere. Fewer than 200,000 troops occupied Indonesia, the Philippines, Malaya and Burma. They depended upon the co-operation of the occupied peoples, and this required concessions such as the freeing of nationalist leaders. For their part, how were the nationalists to regard the Japanese? To view them as liberators would have been naive. The first priority of the Japanese was to win the war. If they did so it was highly likely that Indonesia would merely see Dutch colonialism replaced by Japanese. So, Indonesian nationalists sought guarantees.

Such difficulties caused Japanese-Indonesian relations to break down from late 1942. Some freed nationalists had immediately taken up resistance. The Japanese responded with repression. Resisters commonly found themselves deported as forced labour to Burma. At the same time, the Japanese continued to seek the cooperation of the moderate nationalist leaders such as Sukarno and Hatta. They agreed to take the central role in the Centre of People's Power (PUTERA), but turned it from a vehicle for increasing war production into a mass movement for taking power after the war. The Volunteer Army of the Defenders of the Homeland (PETA), a force of 120,000 raised to fight the Allies, proved equally nationalist after the war.

Occupation proved an ambiguous experience. The Japanese both repressed and conciliated; Indonesians both collaborated and resisted. Nationalists did not want occupation to become merely an exchange of colonialisms, so they took up Japanese offers of participation in the hope that it might lead to no colonialism at all. A further difference was that the Japanese were Asians not Europeans. The Japanese did allow nationalist leaders more political freedom even if for their own ends. The problem was that nationalism proved a powerful genie to let out of colonial bottles. Neither the Japanese nor the Dutch, when they returned after the Second World War, could recapture it.

'The Indies Must Be Free'

'Strengthen our ranks'

d) Dutch Decolonisation

The Japanese resisted independence until the Allies approached Indonesia in June 1945. At that point, they conceded the Jakarta Charter which promised to respect a constitution based upon the five principles of nationalism, internationalism, representative government, social justice, and belief in God. Sukarno then went further and declared independence, which conflicted with the aim of the arriving British and Indian troops to restore the Dutch. The Dutch condemned the Nationalist leaders as collaborators with only minority support, and continued to claim sovereignty. However, international pressure forced the Dutch to negotiate.

Indonesia is geographically a collection of many islands, of which Java was the centre of nationalism. The Nationalists were republicans and refused to remain within a Commonwealth under the Dutch Crown. The Dutch strategy was to defeat nationalism by politically dividing the larger islands from the outlying ones. To achieve this they proposed federal government, thereby exploiting suspicions of Javanese authoritarianism. Once isolated, it was imagined that the Javanese could be brought to the conference table. The Javanese Nationalists were forced to negotiate because of the weakness of their own movement. It represented the Javanese middle classes, and it only became more popular with the mass of non-Javanese peasants when the Dutch used military force against it.

The Dutch used federalism to prevent a unitary state. Consequently they made two separate agreements in 1946. The first was with the 'Malino states' beyond Java. The second, the Linggadjati

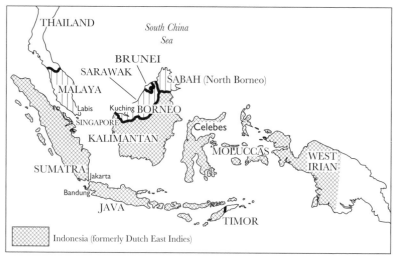

Indonesia (formerly Dutch East Indies)

Treaty, recognised a Republic of Indonesia, consisting of Java and Sumatra. Outlying Borneo and Eastern Indonesia were to be separate states still in union with the Dutch Crown. Founded on mistrust, it was never an arrangement likely to last.

In the Netherlands the Linggadjati Treaty divided the parties. The Catholic Party condemned it as a climbdown. As it fell apart, they and the Army leadership called for military reoccupation which they wrongly assumed would be welcomed by Indonesians. They dismissed Indonesian nationalism as a conspiracy by former collaborators of the Japanese who lacked popular support. Against this, was the argument of the Labour Party that a genuine nationalist revolution had taken place. A limited military presence, only, was required to support moderate against extreme leaders. More than this would not be supported by international opinion, nor was it affordable.

The interventionists prevailed and the first 'police action' of July 1947 was launched. It was designed to bring the Republic's economy to its knees by occupying the valuable rice and oil lands. Foreign trade was cut-off by a naval blockade, causing a refugee crisis. This first intervention failed because the Dutch were too weak to resist international condemnation of their actions at the UNO. By the Renville Agreement of January 1948 they granted the Republic recognition of its independence within a federation of Indonesian states.

Dutch troops were to remain on Republican territory during the twelve months to independence. They were used as nationalist guerrillas stepped-up their activity. Even the once-compliant Malino states now abandoned the Dutch. Dutch belligerence was beginning to alienate crucial allies such as the USA. Despite this the conservative coalition, elected in the summer of 1948, launched a second 'police action'. They were trying to bring about decolonisation on their own terms: a weak federation that the Republic would be unable to control. Yet that Republic had just won the belated respect of the USA by suppressing a communist-led insurgency. Americans reinvented Sukarno, the author of *Nationalism, Islam, and Marxism* (1926), as a Cold War ally.

The Dutch failed to quell people's resistance in the countryside. They wrongly assumed that most Indonesians did not support the Republican leadership. When this was exposed as fallacious, the Corps of Special Troops resorted to restoring control through terror. The bombing of Jakarta shocked international opinion. The consequences of the second action for the Dutch were highly damaging: stronger people's resistance; loss of remaining support from the Malino states; and the threat of withdrawal of all financial and military aid by the USA. The Dutch had overstretched themselves and had little option but to reach a final agreement at the Hague in August 1949. But a federal union under the Dutch Crown could not endure for long. By August 1950 Indonesia had become a unitary state under Javanese direction. Four years later, the union was renounced, ostensibly because the Dutch refused to leave West Irian, where they remained until 1963. Thus, post-colonial relations have been distant. Holland's future was in Europe, to the benefit of the Dutch economy.

e) Assessment: the nature and consequences of Dutch decolonisation

The character of Dutch decolonisation in Indonesia was determined by a combination of internal and external factors. Within Indonesia, the use of military force set up a pattern of counter-reaction and more force, that made decolonisation more difficult. The Dutch used force because they failed, or refused, to recognise that an anti-colonial revolution had taken place in the colony. They employed force without the capacity to sustain it over the long-term. Using force impeded the negotiated settlement favoured by the UNO. Behind the use of force lay the continued profitability of Indonesian agriculture. 'The Dutch ... acted in the belief that independence would be a severe blow to the national economy.'[4]

External influences proved more crucial in determining the timing of decolonisation. President Truman's assessment of Cold War priorities in 1949 was that the Dutch were better employed against the communist threat in Europe than in S.E. Asia. Sukarno's Indonesia was not a danger. It could act as a nationalist bulwark against communism. Indonesian decolonisation is an early example of how Cold War interests could supersede those of decolonisers and decolonised.

For Indonesia the legacy of decolonisation has been several decades of authoritarian government within which the military has played an arbitral role. Original fears that it would become a Javanese, one-party state have been confirmed. In 1967, Sukarno was replaced by General Suharto, until 1998, who established a family dynasty controlling not only government but a large share of the economy. The elite continued to corner the benefits of economic growth as before. Furthermore, in one of history's ironic twists, Indonesia itself became a colonialist state during its brutal occupation of the former Portuguese colony of East Timor between 1975 and 1999.

It has been argued that there is a continuity between the way the Dutch decolonised and the development of an authoritarian state in post-colonial Indonesia. The myth that the liberal Dutch managed one of the more humane decolonisations has been exposed by recent research revealing its brutality. More than 100,000 Indonesians and 6,000 Dutch were killed during the 'police actions' of 1946–9. One writer has even drawn similarities between the behaviour of Dutch soldiers and that of the SS during the Second World War. Another has seen Indonesia as a precursor of Vietnam. On a visit to the former colony in 1995, Queen Beatrix publicly regretted the deaths caused by Dutch colonialism, but withheld the official apology many at home thought was due.[5] The Dutch historical memory is being forced to face up to its colonial past. The embarrassment in Dutch history does not only reside in the consciences of rich, seventeenth-century merchants. It lives on in those of the decolonisers.

3 Belgian Decolonisation of the Congo

a) Belgian colonialism to 1945

King Leopold II of Belgium's admiration for commercial Dutch colonialism fed his ambitions for his own country. He once said, 'There are no small nations, there are only small minds'.[6] Such inverted logic led to the creation of the Congo Free State by 1885, a colony eighty times the size of Belgium, rich in mineral resources, and unique as Leopold's personal fiefdom until 1908. Belgian capital showed little interest until the Crown demonstrated the colony's profitability.

This took some time. Through the 1880s and 1890s, Leopold permitted a brutal colonialism of terror. State officials raided villages for rubber and ivory. If they encountered resistance they kidnapped and ransomed the women and cut off the ears and hands of the men. Other colonial states urged Leopold to put his house in order. In 1908 he made a start by passing the colony over to the state, which invited Belgian capital in. The Crown had opened up the non-ferrous metals of the Katanga region and constructed waterways and railways. Belgian investors hoped colonialism might raise profits that had declined through the Great Depression (1873–96).

Historians have described Belgian administration of the Congo after 1908 as paternalist. Colonial administrators believed in the uncivilised inferiority of their charges. One Governor-General, P. Ryckman, illustrated this by announcing that blacks were two-thousand years behind whites. No African sat on the Governor-General's Council until 1947. Social order was maintained by using compliant chiefs to govern through the tribal networks. By the 1930s this was breaking down as the handful of dominant colonial companies, seeking to attract labour to the mines, began urbanisation. The new towns filled up with mixed tribal populations divorced from their rural roots.

Rapid urbanisation threatened social disorder if it was not carefully controlled. Paternalism in the new urban context was designed to produce a productive, compliant workforce, content with conditions materially better than those found elsewhere in colonial Africa. Three agencies of paternalism made up a triangular power structure to achieve this. The first was the colonial administration. While it remained entirely Belgian in composition, it did deliver welfare policies such as the provision of medical care. Secondly, there were the companies backed by Belgian finance houses. They needed swift improvements in levels of skill and labour productivity. Retention of skilled labour, once trained, was vital and assisted by good company welfare schemes that provided sickness and industrial injury benefits, and retirement pensions. Thirdly, there were the Catholic Church missions. They provided the best primary education in Africa and enjoyed a near-monopoly over Congolese schooling until the 1950s. They reproduced a literate and numerate labour force blessed also with Catholic morality. Peemans has described the Church's behaviour as 'ideological indoctrination' and 'totalitarian'.[7] He argues that the Church's teaching extended beyond the conversion of Africans to Catholicism. It opposed trade unionism as unnecessary because the companies provided welfare.

b) Volatile Decolonisation, 1945–60

Unlike the Dutch, Belgian decolonisation did not appear imminent as the Second World War ended. The Congo had not suffered occupation, and in 1945 seemed to be one of the most stable examples of colonialism. That all this changed with tragic suddenness in 1959–60 illustrates the volatility and unpredictability of decolonisation. Explaining the specific causes of this is, therefore, of great importance. The contrast with Dutch experience is that, although decolonisation was also violent it occurred after decolonisation in the form of a civil war. Post-colonial civil war in the Congo resembles the experience of Portuguese Africa rather than that of the Dutch East Indies. But the post-colonial civil wars in the ex-Portuguese colonies were continuities from the colonial period. This was not the case in the Congo where there had been no war before decolonisation.

World War Two stimulated the Belgian Congo economically, through increasing demand for its raw materials. Unlike Belgium itself the Congo remained uninvaded throughout the war. The Congo's post-war stability depended upon the Belgians' careful management of its economic resources, particularly plentiful in Katanga. The Belgian and international financiers who had invested in the copper and diamond mines opposed any move towards decolonisation. Once the atomic age dawned in 1945, the United States observed that 80 per cent of the world's uranium was located in the Congo.

The social consequences of industrialisation – one-quarter of the population living in urban areas – caused what Peemans has termed the 'Belgianization'[8] of Congolese society. Congolese workers were beginning to behave like Belgian ones. In 1946 the administration could not resist giving trade union rights although it tried to contain militancy through consultative workers' councils. Through the 1950s living standards rose appreciably, particularly in the urban areas. The

Congolese were riding 700,000 bicycles by the end of the decade compared with only 50,000 at its beginning.

'Belgianization' also raised middle-class hopes of upward social mobility. These might express themselves as nationalism if they were not directed towards a career structure. Two ladders leaned towards the window of opportunity. The first was the Catholic Church whose missions reproduced a devout African clergy. The other was the colonial administration. More exclusive than the Church, it operated a 'development policy' that amounted to offering an unofficial quota of black jobs. Many qualified Africans were screened-out through a system of 'personal inspection'. Nevertheless, the fact that any Africans were getting jobs in the administration caused Belgians to fear for theirs.

The rural aspect of 'development policy' set out to create a class of small, independent farmers. African advancement met with obstruction from white settlers who clung to the land, as they did in Kenya and Angola. Frustrated peasants migrated to the towns, adding to a growing surplus of unskilled labour. By the late 1950s 'development policy' had failed to solve the mounting social crisis. Its opponents, white civil servants and farmers, accused the metropole of acting against their interests.

The early Congolese political parties, led by either the urban middle class or rural chieftains, demanded accelerated reforms. King Badouin's sympathetic visit of 1955 gave them hope and the Socialist-Liberal government in Belgium prepared to respond positively. It proposed the extension of state primary education. The Church bitterly resisted this encroachment on its monopoly but its position was undermined by the Vatican. In 1956, the Vatican realised that the price of continued influence in Africa was acceptance of its inevitable independence. In Belgium, the Government was being pressed to propose a specific timescale for decolonisation. French moves in this direction in West Africa were held up as an example.

The first local government elections were held in 1957 and resulted in a majority for the Abako party. Initially, Abako had been based upon the traditional ethnic politics of only the third biggest Congolese tribe, the Bakongo. They wanted reunification of their people who were scattered across three empires: Belgian, French and Portuguese. Under Joseph Kasavubu's leadership it modernised its programme to advocate equal access to education and the administration. This wider appeal enabled it to defeat the parties of the two largest tribes, the Hutus and the Tutsis. Kasavubu called for a general election for 'internal autonomy'. A hasty Belgian blueprint for decolonisation in 1958 failed to defuse the growing crisis.

The catalyst of Belgian decolonisation was the Leopoldville riots of December 1959. They surprised many but are far from being inexplicable. One cause was reduced economic growth. Crawford Young points to the frustration of expectations that this caused.

The Belgian Congo, 1960

> The welfare thrust of the terminal colonial state and its ample resource
> base brought – really for the first time in the colonial era – a tangible,
> broad-based, sustained rise in the level of African well-being, and the
> anticipation of more to come.[9]

But the first wave of industrialisation was over by 1955 and Congolese
mineral exports fell from 1957 causing rising urban unemployment.
This was exacerbated by the flow of rural-urban migration.

Delayed political action in the face of mounting expectations was
the other half of the story. The colonial administration was divided
over Brussels' plan to secularise education. One part favoured it; the
other sided with the Church's opposition and its call to the Catholic
African population to resist it.

On 4 January 1959, an Abako meeting was banned and turned into
attacks upon white property, schools and missions. The riots
continued for two days during which police action killed over a
hundred people. Abako was banned and its leaders arrested. A jour-
nalistic source offered an explanation of why the riots had lasted so
long.

> 1) The Belgian authorities had neither the technique nor suitable equip-
> ment for non-violent intervention. 2) The police forces and the military
> garrison of Leopoldville were numerically very weak ... and were com-
> posed entirely of Africans with the exception of the officers. Moreover
> 5 the police ... were detested and their mere presence merely fanned the
> flames. The Belgian paratroopers ... were only in number when they
> took part on Monday in the control operations and at no time did they
> use their arms. 3) The administrative authorities delayed until the last
> moment the massive intervention of the black 'security force' ... for
> 10 fear of provoking a massacre and with the hope that the riots would
> subside once the looting was over ... the police ... lost its self-control
> more easily than the army.[10]

It is clear that the Belgians were trying to control the African population with African forces (a tactic used even more extensively by the
Portuguese, whose colonial wars began with similar urban rioting in
Angola). Here, they were under-prepared. There was a great reluctance to commit better trained, Belgian paratroopers to riot control
duties. Increasingly frustrated by the continuance of the riots, the
black armed forces ended by over-reacting. From this document, the
historian can certainly detect the kind of attitudes that caused the
Belgians to leave swiftly.

The scale of the spontaneous violence in Leopoldville shocked the
administration. Unlike the Dutch before them, or the Portuguese
after, the Belgian response was to leave as quickly as possible. Some
investors took fright and withdrew, but the big investors remained
and prepared to defend their assets in the new Congo.

d) Decolonisation as 'disembodied statelessness' 1960–64

Fourteen Congolese parties in attendance at Brussels in January 1960 prised from the Belgians a six-month time-scale for independence. Nationalist impatience jeopardised the prospects of a stable transfer of power. Unlike in Indonesia, no anti-colonial organisation of any pedigree existed. The result was disintegration into internecine conflict, as the Belgians sought to pass power over as quickly as possible. It was crisis management in the fast lane.

Immature parties fought the pre-independence elections of May 1960. 'The politicization of ethnicity',[11] as it has been called, was exploited to maximise votes. It exposed the fault lines of Congolese society. The new unitary government was divided like the society it ruled. President Kasavubu had turned Abako into a party based in Leopoldville. Prime Minister Lumumba's Congolese National Alliance was a widespread coalition of peasants and urban workers. Thirdly, Tshombe's Conakat was based in mineral-rich, southern Katanga. The competition to occupy the posts of departing Belgians was frenetic. Other Belgians, like businessmen and missionaries, remained to complicate matters. Decolonisation in a hurry left the Congo in a condition of 'disembodied statelessness'.[12]

Breakdown began with the new army flexing its muscles by insisting upon the dismissal of all remaining Belgian officers. The Belgians responded by evacuating all their nationals. Having appeased the army the government attended to the high salary demands of the political class. They were to be met through high taxation of prosperous Katanga. Tshombe's Conakat refused the bill and seceded from the new state. Ethnic differences amplified expression of this economic conflict. Katangans condemned Leopoldville as the home of a new colonialism. Civil war marked the second stage of the disembodiment of the new state. Katangan secession was supported by mining companies alarmed by the Leopoldville government's threats of nationalisation. However, P.H. Spaak (Belgium's Foreign Minister) convinced the companies that Belgium should play a conciliatory role and that Katangan secession was unacceptable to the international community.

The third stage of disembodiment was the division of the Leopoldville-based state into civil conflict. Lumumba was dismissed as Prime Minister by Kasavubu after a failed invasion of Katanga in 1962. He then established a rival base in Stanleyville. As the Americans backed Leopoldville, Lumumba invited Soviet support to restore the balance of power. Two factors undermined their intervention, however. Lumumba was captured by the Leopoldville government and cynically handed over to the Katangans for execution. Secondly, the United Nations, anxious about the Congo becoming a Cold War arena, intervened.

United Nations' intervention had some success. By January 1963,

Katanga was reconciled by the offer of a federal system of government, under President Cyrille Adoula. In addition, the army was reorganised under General Mobutu. Tshombe himself became Prime Minister in 1964 when economic stagnation and bureaucratic corruption caused a further collapse of law and order. The last pockets of resistance around Stanleyville were then crushed.

d) Post-colonial hang-overs

Peace did not deliver political stability to the new Democratic Republic of Congo (Zaire from 1971). In 1965 Mobutu took power through a coup. Over three decades his dictatorship ransacked the state to the point of collapse, hardly distinguishing between the state's and his own family's expenditure. However, the collapse of world copper prices in 1990 reduced a personal income that the World Bank estimated had been worth $400 million per year through the 1980s. On Mobutu's fall in 1997, much Zairean opinion blamed the West.

1 The United States and the West are also despised for standing by while
   a nation suffered three decades of assault and robbery. During the Cold
   War years they turned a blind eye to President Mobutu's excesses
   because he was seen as a buffer against the spread of communism in
5 Africa, and in particular, in neighbouring Angola. Only when the cold
   war ended did human rights matter. But by then President Mobutu had
   amassed a fortune and Zaire was spent.[13]

Mobutu was forced from power by the Democratic Alliance forces of Laurent Kabila, a former associate of Lumumba's. Zaire has again become the Democratic Republic of Congo, but civil war drawing in several neighbouring states continued into 2000.

Peemans has argued that decolonisation, far from freeing Belgium from her former colony, left her with an 'imperial hang over.'[14] Beyond 1960 Belgian companies remained heavily invested in Zaire in neo-colonial relationships. These, and the continuance of governmental aid to the Mobutu dictatorship, were heavily criticised by the radical sectors of the Belgian public. On balance, Peemans considers the Belgian economy lost more than it gained from post-colonial investment in Zaire. This was because it could have invested more profitably elsewhere in the global economy, notably in Europe.

e) Assessment: Belgian decolonisation as a 'self-righting model'?

R.F. Holland has argued that the Congo provides the historian with a 'self-righting' model of decolonisation by which colonies move from dependency to a new, independent equilibrium via internal discord. First, there takes place a transfer of power from colonialists to indigenous elites. Secondly, these elites come into conflict with one another. Thirdly, this conflict is ended through necessary compromise. Finally, a stable government emerges which is not only satisfactory to the indigenous parties, but also to the decolonising power and to any interested superpower.

Stages one to three of the 'self-righting' model are applicable to the Congo to 1965. Problems arise with the final stage. Mobutu's overthrow in 1997, by an opposition that had spent thirty years in an isolated eastern enclave, shows his regime was never satisfactory to all indigenous parties. More accurately, it satisfied the needs of the West through the Cold War. But all models exclude, by definition, unique characteristics. Certain differences stand out when comparing the Congo with the previous example of Indonesia. Firstly, international capital played an obstructive role in the Congo. A colony's economic resources, therefore, can pattern its decolonisation (see the case of Angola later in this chapter). Secondly, periodisation also patterns decolonisations because the international context changes through time. The Belgians left hurriedly in 1960 very conscious of the French war in Algeria and of the failure of the Dutch to recolonise Indonesia. But, by the 1960s, decolonisation had become a Cold War issue in a way that it had hardly been from 1945 to1955. Thirdly, rapid departures, however much demanded, do not necessarily make for stable decolonisations. One may, therefore, be tempted to argue the opposite: that careful planning makes for peaceful transfers of power. Unfortunately, the case of India (see Chapter 3) gives the lie to such complacent conclusions.

4 The Last to Leave: Portuguese Decolonisation

> **KEY ISSUE** Why was Portuguese decolonisation so late and so violent? How exceptional was it?

a) The Myth of Exceptionalism: Portugal's Colonial Mission

Until 1974 Portugal was a dictatorship, not a parliamentary democracy like Holland, Belgium, Britain or France. The nationalist Portuguese dictatorship was intensely proud of its colonialism. It believed it had an exceptional historic mission to civilise the peoples it had colonised in Africa and Asia from the fifteenth century onwards. The colonies were celebrated as 'the Discoveries', as if the sole purpose of their historical existence was for the Portuguese to find them. Just one year before the colonial wars began the dictator Salazar built at Belém in Lisbon a Monument to the Discoveries. It commemorates the five-hundredth anniversary of the death of Prince Henry the Navigator in 1560. His figure points majestically westwards, down the magnificent vista that is the estuary of the River Tagus, to the Atlantic Ocean and the world beyond. Few pieces of modern

European sculpture capture a nation's ideology so evocatively and with such a sense of place. Other nations might colonise for gain; Portugal had a Christian mission to save souls. It was God's own work.

But Salazar's timing was badly out. Just after the Monument was completed, India invaded the territory of Goa (1961). Portugal had first colonised it in 1510. Prime Minister Nehru of India simultaneously rejected the myth of Portugal's special mission and exposed its military weakness. Africa paid the price for the loss of Goa. Salazar blamed the army which responded by tenaciously defending its honour and the empire. This led to a decade and a half of colonial wars as a result of which the regime destroyed itself. The national liberation movements in the African colonies failed to win complete military victory. But they had always said that the regime would never decolonise, it must fall first. It fell, at the instigation of disaffected officers of the Armed Forces Movement on 25 April 1974.

The Portuguese Revolution that replaced dictatorship with democracy was an almost entirely peaceful affair. The blood had been spilled in Africa before. By 1976 the entire empire, except Macau, was gone. It passed from history like all the other European empires. There seems nothing exceptional about that. The great bridge over the Tagus was renamed, like many public places, to commemorate the Revolution. *Ponte 25 de Abril* (Bridge of 25 April) is exceptional in its length. At 2,278 metres (approximately 1½ miles) it takes at least half-an-hour to walk across. To understand why the bridge to revolution and subsequent decolonisation proved such a long one, we must first examine the nature of the colonial system passed on to the Salazar regime by its predecessors.

b) From Mission to Paradise Lost: the Reality of Portuguese Colonialism

The Empire was given a new lease of life by the Berlin Conference of 1884, by which the colonial powers reached a measure of agreement about the division of their African teritiories. Despite what Portuguese governments said economic motives were usually more important than religious ones in colonial policy. Because Portuguese capitalism was under-developed the colonial economy was used to support the domestic one. But the colonial economy itself could not be successfully developed by poor Portugal alone.

This was why the Republic (1910–26) liberalised colonial policy by allowing foreign investment into the colonies. It was the monopolists in Portugal, previously protected in their colonial enterprises from foreign competition, who suffered a fall in trade and profits. They were behind the military coup which overthrew the Republic. But the junior officers proved disastrous economists. They were compelled to call in a civilian academic to balance the books. By the 1933 Constitution, Antonio de Oliveira Salazar announced a 'New State'

(*Estado Novo*) in Portugal. Already, in 1930, his Colonial Act had imposed central state control over the colonies and their economies. Once again, the colonies were heavily protected, deemed to exist to benefit the metropole. Their trading profits were to be used to build up Lisbon's gold and foreign exchange reserves. The colonial budget was rigorously balanced and the money supply limited. The colonial monopolists and landowners, whose privileges had been eroded under the Republic, were delighted with the protection Salazarism gave them.

Gervase Clarence-Smith, in *The third Portuguese empire 1825–1975*, argues that the colonial policy of the *Estado Novo* in the 1930s became more racist because it was influenced by fascism. Salazarism did go through a fascist period, but the Colonial Act looked back to the practice of the monarchy before 1910. Portuguese colonialism had always been racist. Below the (white) Portuguese, the official classification divided Africans into 'civilised' and 'natives'. The categories were not immutable; one could become 'civilised' by demonstrating the ability to speak Portuguese, financial self-sufficiency and 'appropriate conduct'. Only a small minority bothered.

The Colonial Act was reformed in 1951 because of anti-colonial pressure fom the United Nations. Portugal redesignated all its colonies 'overseas provinces'. Their peoples were granted full Portuguese citizenship in 1961, but these cosmetic changes came too late to save colonialism.

Another example of colonial racism is the lack of education, which Salazar distrusted as potentially subversive. African illiteracy rates in the early 1960s were above 90 per cent. But it was forced labour that epitomised the harshness of Portuguese colonialism. Africans were obliged to work for the state for nothing to build ports, railways and roads. Basil Davidson observes in *The African Awakening* (1955), how it took men away from their villages and families, sometimes resulting in the women and children left behind having to substitute forced labour in their home regions. But forced labour was not introduced by the *Estado Novo*. It was another continuity from the monarchy (1899).

A neglected aspect of Portuguese colonialism is its propaganda. The Salazar regime was highly successful in sanitising its policies for international consumption. The Portuguese have a phrase '*para ingles ver*' which means 'for the English to see', or as the English would say 'to pull the wool over the eyes', (it originates from the days when Portuguese slave traders hid their illegal cargoes from prying English boarders). The Ministry of Information's job was also to deceive, the English and anyone else. It found a friend in the Brazilian sociologist Gilberto Freyre whose theory of Luso-Tropicalism argued the Portuguese had a unique genius for evolving non-racist, multi-cultural societies. The Guinean nationalist Amilcar Cabral exposed this fiction with devastating sarcasm:

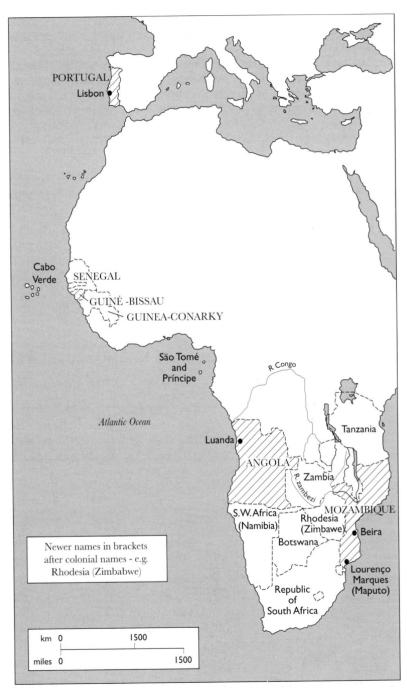

The Portuguese Empire in Africa

1   the fascist colonialism of Portugal took care to suppress all means of
non-official information about its 'overseas provinces'. A powerful
propaganda machine was put to work at convincing international opinion that our people lived in the best of all possible worlds, depicting
5   happy Portuguese 'of colour' whose only pain was the yearning for their
white mother-country, so sadly torn from them by the facts of geogra-
phy. A whole mythology was assembled ... even a renowned Sociologist
... Gilberto Freyre transformed all of us who live in the colony-
10 provinces of Portugal into the fortunate inhabitants of a Luso-Tropical
paradise.[15]

However, as Portuguese gun-fire was turned upon urban African pro-
testors at the end of 1960, there was clearly trouble in paradise, and
nationalists like Cabral were losing their sense of humour. So too was
the historian Charles Boxer, Professor of Portuguese at King's
College, London, who replied to Freyre's views in his book *Race
Relations in the Portuguese Colonial Empire 1415–1825* (1963). In it he
argued that the Portuguese had discriminated against non-white
people throughout their imperial history. This was not what the
Salazar regime wanted to hear and it entered into a propaganda war
against Boxer who received masses of hate-mail, much of which probably came from the Portuguese Secret Police.

c) Colonial Wars and the Portuguese Revolution, 1961–75

Portuguese decolonisation is perhaps the best example of the usefulness of a triangular model of decolonisation. Nationalism, the decline
of the metropole and Cold War superpower politics fused together as
causes. The colonial wars split Portuguese society, eventually causing
a political revolution. The involvement of the superpowers in the wars
has led some historians to argue that they were more than colonial
wars. Like Vietnam, they should be seen as a part of the Cold War.
The Portuguese encouraged such an interpretation by arguing that
the wars were caused by a united communist conspiracy that was using
African nationalism for its own ends. While this was an exaggeration
typical of Portuguese propaganda, and the wars did have their own
separate characters, it was not without evidence. The leading
nationalist parties all claimed to be fighting a people's anti-colonial
war to establish socialism.

Patrick Chabal's work points towards four differences between
Portuguese decolonisation and those of the other European
powers. Firstly, it was the last major European evacuation. It took
some fifteen years of war during which intense superpower rivalry
both complicated and prolonged decolonisation. Secondly, it was
achieved through people's war. This produced a close and active
relationship between party and people that made the post-colonial
state likely to be participatory, even democratic. Thirdly, much
nationalism was socialist, often Marxist. Leaders adopted the

Chinese, Cubans and Vietnamese as models of liberation not least because aid sprang from those sources. However, the weaknesses of their own economies made them ultimately dependent upon the capitalist world market, and this made socialism impossible. Fourthly, decolonisation could only be achieved through metropolitan revolution. This was because Portugal was unique amongst the colonial powers in being a dictatorship that refused to decolonise. Unlike in the democracies, the dictatorial regime had to be replaced first.

Despite obvious similarities the wars in each colony should be seen as distinct. The war in Angola was characterised by conflict between the three principal nationalist groups. The MPLA was a modern party, strong in the urban areas around the capital Luanda, and led by Lisbon-educated Marxists like Agostinho Neto with strong links to the communist opposition. The FNLA was more traditional. Suspicious of socialism as a foreign doctrine it drew upon a rural constituency, the Bakongo tribe, who lived either side of the Congolese border. It was led by Holden Roberto, a Baptist who had lived most of his life in the Congo and was profoundly influenced by decolonisation there. After splitting from the FNLA, Jonas Savimbi formed UNITA in 1966, building what Chabal calls 'ethno-nationalism', a power base amongst his own ethnic group, the Ovimbundu. Later, UNITA broadened its appeal.

The Angolan rising began in early 1962 with separate attacks by the MPLA in Luanda and the FNLA in the north. In this early stage, the FNLA was the most effective party but splits in the late 1960s enabled the MPLA to supersede it as the dominant influence. However, the MPLA itself divided in the early 1970s enabling the Portuguese to regain ascendancy. A further complication was added by Chinese assistance to the FNLA, even though it was not Marxist, because their ideological rivals the USSR were assisting the MPLA.

The absence of nationalist unity, and the failure of any party to set up genuinely autonomous areas, enabled the Portuguese to fight a successful counter-insurgency campaign. Because fighting was kept away from the most populated areas economic growth continued. The number of white settler emigrants actually doubled through the 1960s. A rural reorganisation policy penned populations into strategic hamlets (*aldeamentos*). Guerrilla strongholds were bombed with napalm and herbicides. Military strategy was modelled partly on the British experience in Malaya – Portuguese officers had been trained in Britain – and partly on American tactics in Vietnam. Psychological warfare was employed to exploit nationalist divisions. But many Angolans fought for the Portuguese. Over forty per cent of their armed forces were Africans. For all these reasons there was no nationalist victory in Angola.

The contrasts with Guinea-Bissau could hardly be greater. The

Portuguese came to regard it as expendable for two reasons. Firstly, it lacked the mineral wealth of Angola. Secondly, the population was small, around 10 per cent of Angola's, and contained very few white settlers. Portugal's weaker commitment to Guinea was further drained by the quality of its indigenous politics. Guinean nationalism combined in a single, coherent movement PAIGC, and was blessed with outstanding political leadership. Under Amilcar Cabral in 1963–64, PAIGC fought a successful guerrilla war that restricted the Portuguese to fortified areas that they could only defend through superior air power. However, from 1973, PAIGC obtained Soviet surface-to-air missiles which shifted the balance towards it. By the autumn, PAIGC's declaration of independence had been recognised by a number of members of the UNO. This was no mean achievement, as Cabral's biographer notes.

1   His party, the PAIGC, was the most successful nationalist movement in Black Africa and the first to achieve independence through armed struggle. It did so by mobilising the villagers of Guinea into a political and military force capable of challenging Portuguese colonial rule; and it went
5   some way towards establishing a new social and political order in areas which it wrested from Portuguese control. The PAIGC's achievements were very largely due to Cabral's leadership.[16]

PAIGC set out to establish a 'new social and political order' through control of autonomous areas. Though it fell short of socialism the new order was participatory. Despite professing socialist objectives Cabral kept Guinea non-aligned. This avoided alienating the NATO powers while retaining Soviet support. Guinea largely escaped Angola's subjection to Cold War politics. Portugal responded late to Cabral's political mastery through General Antonio de Spinola's 'for a better Guinea' campaign. Convinced by Vietnam that guerrilla wars could not be won by the colonial power, Spinola targeted the 'hearts and minds' of the people through educational, health and political reforms. It was too late, their hearts and minds were already with PAIGC. Cabral's assassination in 1973, by a dissident PAIGC member probably working with the Portuguese secret police (PIDE), did nothing to win them back.

Spinola was always trying to catch up with history. By the time his *Portugal and the Future* was published (February 1974), arguing for a Lusophone commonwealth to replace empire, an Armed Forces Movement (MFA) of dissident officers was already planning the coup of 25 April. Service in Guinea had convinced leaders like Major Otelo Saraiva de Carvalho that complete decolonisation was the only solution.

After divided beginnings, the nationalist war in Mozambique ended by resembling Guinean unity. Great ethnic diversity impeded nationalism and the the main party, FRELIMO, was only set up with considerable external assistance from Tanzania. Internal conflicts resulted in the assassination of its first leader, Eduardo Mondlane, and in the Portuguese being able to contain the conflict. From 1970, however, it regrouped under the united leadership of Samora Machel. From safe homes in Tanzania and Malawi the war was extended to new regions. The Portuguese army, 70 per cent African, could no longer guarantee the safety of its settlers. Terror and *aldeamentos* became its last resorts. By the time of the Revolution (25 April 1974) FRELIMO was confident of victory, not least because of aid from the USSR and Cuba, whose Marxism they shared.

Mozambique illustrates how complicated decolonisation in Africa could be by the 1960s. Mozambican decolonisation was delayed until 1975 by the special problems of Southern Africa. It was the only Portuguese colony with hostile white regimes as neighbours. From 1965, the illegal Rhodesia, which depended for its oil supplies upon a pipeline running through Mozambique, joined South Africa as a hostile power. Portuguese control of Mozambique was strategically important in maintaining white power in Southern Africa. The West sympathised with the Portuguese domino theory that if white power collapsed it would be replaced by black communism. A good example of the way the Portuguese exploited this position to defend their colonialism is the financing of the Cabora Bassa hydro-electric dam. The South Africans, as the principal beneficiaries, were the biggest investors. But European capital was also attracted and, thus, gained an interest in the survival of Portuguese colonialism.

d) Consequences of Decolonisation: Post-Colonial Lusophone Africa and Portugal

The hopes of Marxists in the 1970s that people's wars would produce Africa's first revolutionary socialist states have been disappointed. The Lusophone states are today searching for an African path. The socialist model is no longer open to them, but neither should they be judged to have 'failed' by a capitalist model either. The standards of the West or the former Soviet bloc were never real post-colonial options. Neither do the long civil wars in Angola and Mozambique imply an African 'failure' of self-government. A history of violence is a continuity inherited from the Portuguese, and the Portuguese and their allies left unfinished Cold War business after the 1974 Revolution. Cabral once wisely said that decolonisation does not end with the withdrawal of the colonisers. He identified neo-colonialism – the continuing, informal power of the former colonialists – as the next enemy.

Guinea became independent in August 1974; Angola and Mozambique in 1975. Angola immediately fell into civil war between the rival nationalist parties. In 1992 internationally supervised elections confirmed the MPLA government in power. Savimbi's UNITA took until 1994 to accept them, but continues to resist integration into a unified state. Mozambique has found a more stable peace since 1994. As apartheid collapsed in South Africa so too did sponsorship of RENAMO, the anti-FRELIMO force in Mozambique.

Examiners are fond of asking the old chestnut about whether decolonisation brought any more than independence for the new states. The devastation wrought by civil war in Angola and Mozambique makes it tempting to answer that it did not. But the bigger question is why did civil war succeed colonial war and persist? The answer is not to be found in racist reductions about 'tribalism' or mystical language about Africa being a 'Dark Continent.', but in politics. Through the 1980s the international community failed post-colonial Lusophone Africa. Only once European communism collapsed between 1989 and 1991 did Africa's international position as pawn in the Cold War end. Only when Nelson Mandela completed his 'long walk to freedom' in 1994 did the African context change fundamentally. Today, Mozambique is at peace, but Angola's conflicts go on fuelled by the diamond trade that buys the arms. War has outlived ideology, for the fighting is no longer about socialist planning or free market economics. Mozambique's peace, by contrast, has attracted development aid and has brought rising living standards. The next generation of post-colonial historians must decide if this is due more to capitalism or the absence of war.

How has decolonisation changed the former colonial power? The Revolution of 1974 was made for a new Portugal: Eurocentric and democratic. The rejection of a colonial in favour of a European future made further progress with entry into the EEC in 1986. Economically, Portugal has not looked back. Democratic Portugal has faced up to its post-colonial responsibilities and struggled to repair the damage inflicted by the dictatorship. In Portugal, if not in Africa, decolonisation has produced a nation at peace with itself. Lisbon is today a multicultural city like Amsterdam or Brussels, and black Portuguese come to view the Monument to the Discoveries alongside white. They are thankful that the colonial mission is over because the paradise promised seemed more like hell. Yet, wounds have healed and Portugal and Africa are still together. The Tagus carries different cargo since the days when Salazar venerated the memory of Henry the Navigator. It no longer flows with the blood of Africa, but Africa's blood still flows.

5 Conclusions

The decolonisations of the smaller European powers clearly have causes common to those of Britain and France: the effects of war; the rise of nationalism; decline of the metropole; the changing world economy; and international relations dominated by Cold War. Yet, on close comparison their substantial differences make R.F. Holland's four-stage, 'self-righting' model, put forward in 1985, appear too

ANTONIO DE OLIVEIRA SALAZAR (1889–1970)

Leadership can be a crucial part of an answer to questions about why some decolonisations had different outcomes to others. The policies pursued by the Portuguese dictator delayed decolonisation.

Salazar was born on 28 April 1889, in the hamlet of Vimieiro in the Dão valley region of Northern Portugal, eight days after Adolf Hitler was born in Austria. The son of a poor bailiff on the local estate, his intelligence took him to the University of Coimbra from where he obtained a doctorate in economics. He became a lecturer there in 1914 and a professor by the age of twenty-seven. Inheriting deep religious beliefs from his parents, he became a leading figure in Catholic politics at Coimbra. In 1928 he became Finance Minister in the military government. He quickly balanced the national budget and abolished the country's foreign debt. By 1932 he was Prime Minister and he remained the effective dictator of Portugal until 1968. Portugal under Salazar was called a 'New State' (*Estado Novo*). It is better described as a one-party state similar to Mussolini's Italy, Hitler's Germany and Franco's Spain.

As we have seen, Salazar spent millions of *escudos* and thousands of lives opposing decolonisation. In 1968, he had a fall whilst undergoing treatment from his chiropodist, causing a stroke and incapacitation. He died two years later still thinking he was Prime Minister because his Cabinet colleagues visited his bedside regularly and never told him otherwise.

The Portuguese Ministry of Information propagandised Salazar's thoughts on colonialism through a series of pamphlets called '*Salazar Says*'. Edited extracts from the series are presented below.

'Salazar Says'
a) about colonialism

Salazar saw his colonialism as being informed by high ideals. He defined colonisation as

> a process of enhancing the economic values of territories administered as colonies, as well as the successive rise of the respective populations to higher forms of social intercourse and government. (*The World Scene and National Problems*, 1957)

b) about Goa

Salazar's Catholicism caused him to identify strongly with the missionary character of Portuguese colonialism. Defending Portugal's colony Goa, as it was challenged by India, he said if world opinon was turning against Portugal then it was

> misguided sensibility ... sentimental revolt ... as if it would be better for large segments of mankind to continue vegetating amidst the primitiveness of their unhappy conditions. (*Portugal and its Overseas Provinces*, 1953).

After India took Goa in 1961 Salazar condemned the Indian Prime Minister in a clever piece of reverse colonialism

> Pandit Nehru ... is the greatest representative of this imperialistic idea ... however strange it may seem to those who listen to his lectures, the Indian Prime Minister is a racist, prejudiced against the West, a pacifist in theory but an aggressor in practice. Not
> 5 only in Asia either. He is beset by the problems of excess population and misery and he has plans for an empty Africa where he hopes that the Indian will be able to take the white man's place. (*The Invasion and Occupation of Goa by the Indian Union*, 1962)

c) about Africa

He predicted only two alternatives for Africa: either the continuation of colonialism; or ruin, degradation and strife. Portugal should be prepared to shed blood to prevent the latter.

> This is our destiny, this is the mission of our life, which we should not curse but rather bless for its loftiness and nobility... [Pro-decolonisers may well] come to think that we did a great service to mankind ... having spared them new forms of slavery. (*Portugal*
> 5 *and the Anti-colonialist Campaign*, 1960)

d) about decolonisation and the Cold War

From a speech to his party, the National Union.

> The West's policy during the second world war made it possible for Russia to take over large tracts of territory in Europe and led to the Communist regime being imposed on several states ... [while the newly independent Asian states] are still profoundly
> 5 rancouring against, or riddled with hate for Western civilization and the White Man, who generously bore it there ... [at a time when Africa] is starting to ... burn in the fire of movements which, incapable of being nationalistic and, only with great difficulty, ideological, are put forward as being racial, in the broadest sense of the
> 10 term. As in Asia, they are too ready to deny the White Man all his civilizing effort and the rights derived therefrom.

> Fearing the Cold War could be lost in the colonial world Salazar anticipated Macmillan in warning
>
> > A wind of uprising is blowing in various parts of Africa ... [whilst Europe was suffering] collective cowardice ... ashamed of the work she has done there ... and ... has unfortunately lost the courage to affirm its superiority. (*Notes on the International Situation*, 1956)
>
> **e)** about the USA and the UNO
>
> Salazar lamented the lack of support Portugal received from the USA and the UNO for its 'mission.' He pointed out that Hawaii was further away from the rest of the USA than the Cape Verde islands were from Portugal:
>
> > according, then, to the theory which tends to evaluate national sovereignty by distances we are not so badly placed ... [Meanwhile] The General Assembly of the United Nations works like a crowd and it is therefore ruled by those psychological laws and that emo-
> > 5 tional atmosphere that govern all crowds ... [behind it lay] an intense campaign of international calumny, skilfully directed by communist Russia ... (*The Portuguese Overseas Territories and the United Nations Organization*, 1961)

mechanistic and complacent. For example, twenty-five years on from decolonisation Angola has still not 'righted-itself' into stable, internationally accepted government, and the Congo is once again engulfed in a war drawing in neighbouring states. Instead we need a more flexible comparison of decolonisations which allows for differences between them. Four factors stand out when viewing the process from a European pespective.

Firstly, periodisation or timing. Dutch decolonisation came a decade earlier than Belgian. The crucial cause was the Second World War which had changed colonial relationships more profoundly in Asia than Africa. Portuguese Africa was even less changed by war than the Belgian Congo, due to Portuguese neutrality. This placed it firmly in the late category. Secondly, speed. The Belgians learned their own lesson from previous experiences like those of the Dutch: leave rapidly. The Portuguese thought they could stand against the tide of history. Thirdly, violence. All three decolonisations were violent but there were degrees of difference. The Dutch employed coercion as a tactic of decolonisation. The Belgians refused it, but an unpredictably rapid escalation of violence occurred after decolonisation. The Portuguese deployment of force greatly exceeded that of the Dutch, or even the French, causing unique people's wars of decolonisation.

Finally, effects upon the metropole. For all European powers decolonisation brought adjustments within their political systems. For the Netherlands and Belgium these were minor. No political system except that of the Portuguese was brought down by decolonisation. In this, it resembled most closely the change from the Fourth to the Fifth Republic in France. The Portuguese regime fell because, as a dictatorship, it lacked the flexibility to deal with the process in the manner of the democracies. Portugal, like the other powers, turned towards European markets and the EEC after decolonisation.

References

1 Simon Schama, *The Embarrassment of Riches* (Fontana, 1987), p.34.
2 Grimal, *Decolonization*, p.84.
3 Grimal, *Decolonization*, p.90.
4 Waites, *Europe and the Third World*, p.248.
5 Paul Doolan, 'Time for Dutch Courage in Indonesia', *History Today, vol. 47(3)*, March 1997, pp.3–5.
6 Roger Anstey, 'The Congo under Leopold', *History of the Twentieth Century, vol. 1* (Purnell, 1968), p.313.
7 Jean-Philippe Peemans, 'Imperial Hangovers: Belgium – The Economics of Decolonization', *Journal of Contemporary History, vol.15*, 1980, p.263.
8 Peemans, *Imperial Hangovers*, p.271.
9 Crawford Young, 'The Colonial State and Post-Colonial Crisis', in Gifford and Louis, *Decolonization and African Independence*, p.25
10 'Esprit', March 1959; quoted in Grimal, *Decolonization*, p.401.
11 Hargreaves, *Decolonization in Africa*, p.178.
12 Holland, *European Decolonization*, p.183.
13 Mary Braid, *The Independent*, 17 May 1997.
14 Peemans, *Imperial Hangovers*, pp.282–3.
15 Basil Davidson, *The Liberation of Guiné* (Penguin 1969), foreward by Amilcar Cabral, p.9.
16 Patrick Chabal, *Amilcar Cabral: Revolutionary leadership and people's war* (Cambridge University Press, 1983), p.2.

Summary Diagram
Comparative Decolonisations

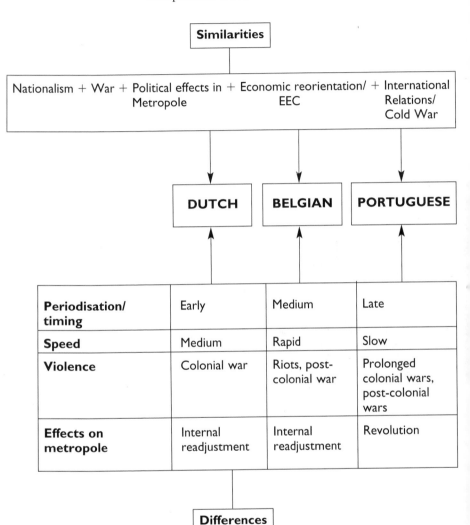

Similarities

Nationalism + War + Political effects in + Economic reorientation/ + International
Metropole EEC Relations/
Cold War

DUTCH **BELGIAN** **PORTUGUESE**

	DUTCH	BELGIAN	PORTUGUESE
Periodisation/ timing	Early	Medium	Late
Speed	Medium	Rapid	Slow
Violence	Colonial war	Riots, post-colonial war	Prolonged colonial wars, post-colonial wars
Effects on metropole	Internal readjustment	Internal readjustment	Revolution

Differences

Answering Source-based questions on Chapter 5

1 Indonesian posters

For each of the two posters 'The Indies must be free' (p.94) and 'Strengthen our ranks' (p.95) answer the following questions.

a) How do the actions of the two figures communicate the messages of the posters? (*4 marks*)

b) Which types of people in particular is each of the posters aimed at? (*4 marks*)

c) How can we tell that each poster was made at a different stage of Indonesian decolonisation? (*4 marks*)

d) Which important aspects of Indonesian decolonisation do the posters describe and which do they leave out? (*8 marks*)

2 'Salazar Says'

Read the profile of Salazar on pp. 115–117 and answer the questions below.

a) Identify the main ideas that run through the linked extracts (*4 marks*)

b) What evidence is there that Salazar saw Portugal as being in an exceptional position in the world? (*4 marks*)

c) Refer back to page 7 (Post-colonial theory: 'decolonising the mind'). Comment on the effects this 'discourse of colonialism' might have upon the thinking of Portuguese and African people? (*5 marks*)

d) What other consequences did Salazar's ideas have for Portuguese decolonisation? (*7 marks*)

6 Conclusions

POINTS TO CONSIDER

You should use the conclusions to reach a broad overview of the three main concerns of the book. Firstly, what were the causes of decolonisation? Secondly, what were its principal characteristics? Thirdly, what have been its main consequences?

1 Causes

KEY ISSUES To what extent was there a common process of decolonisation? How do historians agree and disagree about its principal causes?

The triangular model in the summary diagram at the end of this chapter shows how the effects of world war upon metropoles, nationalism and international relations combined to produce the end of empires. To this extent there was a common process at work. On the other hand, however, each case was different because each example of decolonisation had its own specific characteristics.

From the beginning of the Second World War all the five metropoles written about underwent comparative decline compared with the USA and the USSR. The internal and external growth of these superpowers was enormous. The survival of colonial empires became incompatible with the Cold War and, in Ferro's view, new kinds of imperialism emanated from the USA and the USSR. Internally, the empires were undergoing changes, brought about by economic and social development, that empowered nationalism. The Second World War enhanced this process. But nationalism did not grow uniformly, evolving earlier in Asia than in Africa. Once the superpowers began to make decolonisation their battlefield during the Cold War, it was frequently delayed. This was because these ideological conflicts were never quickly or easily resolved. The Third World bloc of decolonised states, that emerged from the late 1950s, had only limited success in using the UNO to combat such superpower meddling.

If this was the common process, what were the differences? The Second World War weakened colonialism in Asia, where nationalism was stronger, more than in Africa. But even in Asia there were differences. Indians and Pakistanis gained independence before Vietnamese not only because of the relative strengths of their nationalisms, but also due to the different attitudes of the metropoles. Britain was reconciled to decolonisation before France, who fought to recolonise. Both sought to use the colonies to reconstruct the metro-pole's economy. But whereas Britain concentrated upon Africa for this, France sought to keep the whole empire 'assimilated'. The Dutch behaved similarly to the French. The Belgians encountered no challenge from Congolese nationalism until late, and then collapsed in chaos before it. The Portuguese African Empire saw most continu-ity until the early 1960s. But even it could not withstand the wind of change that was sweeping across the continent by then.

Within metropoles important economic changes occurred after the war that propelled decolonisation. By the 1950s, the European market was becoming an alternative vehicle of growth to the colonial one. Even in backward Portugal a pro-European group had begun to recognise this. Belgium, the Netherlands and France had been three of the six founder members of the European Economic Community (EEC) in 1957. Waites argues that France provides the best example of European integration acting as a cause of decolonisation. The British case is not so straightforward. A member of the smaller European Free Trade Association (EFTA) from 1960, Britain did not join the EEC until 1973, having failed with two applications in the 1960s. By 1973 most decolonisation was complete. Nevertheless, the earlier attempts show Britain's intent to change economic direction. Waites believes that decolonisation freed European economies to enjoy their most sustained period of growth of the century.

Holland broadly agrees with Waites that European economic motives lay behind decolonisation. For him a crucial development gap occurred after 1950. Metropoles were modernising faster than their colonies, causing the former to want to end empires. The realis-ation that colonial markets were of declining value compared with the developed world was the key factor. In this view, the 'neo colonialist' argument, that metropoles had found other ways of exploiting colonies, misses the point. Ex-colonies were pushed aside because they were of declining value. All that remained to be done was to ring-fence them from communism. Cain and Hopkins take a more positive view of what the British intended to leave behind. For them, with-drawal came only after capital markets had been well established in the colonies. They agree with Waites that 'neo-colonialism' underes-timates the degree of economic independence ex-colonies were able to achieve.

Ferro too finds 'neo-colonialism' too narrow an explanation. He locates the root causes of decolonisation in the growth of the global economy after 1945 that made the protectionist policies of colonial-ism obsolete. The new global economic system was 'multinational imperialism'.[1] It was dominated by institutions such as the World Bank and the International Monetary Fund that made the whole world the oyster of the richest nations that controlled them.

For Darwin, such grand theories fall into the trap of assuming too much intention. From his study of British imperialism he argues that it had no logic, little system, no uniformity or unity. Decolonisation was a series of miscalculations and anyone claiming otherwise is guilty of 'a picturesque invention ...'² Still, he concedes that it occurred because of the breakdown of international conditions favouring empires. The USA and USSR, both isolationist before the Second World War, emerged to recast the fragments of shattered Japanese imperialism. Like Ferro, he sees after 1945 not the end of imperialism as such, but the transference of its centre to the USSR.

Betts shares Darwin's views about decolonisation not being a process. In *France and Decolonisation* (1991) he saw it as no more than a series of disparate acts that modernised the colonies. Later, however, in *Decolonization* (1998), he describes quite a sophisticated process, identifying nationalism as a main decolonising force. Colonialism steadily developed an urban, market society modeled on Europe. In so doing it reproduced Europe's class society and its discontents. The creation of a colonised bourgeoisie produced the very class that would overthrow colonialism. But, as Gifford and Louis remind us, 'Anti-colonialism was more of a unifying force than nationalism',³ and the two should not be confused. Post-colonial societies usually replaced one type of elite rule by another. 'And the pattern was always of urban elites dominating the countryside.

2 Key Questions Answered

a) Why did decolonisation accelerate so rapidly after 1945?

Decolonisation accelerated so rapidly after 1945 because the Second World War produced new circumstances that were unfavourable to it. Firstly, metropoles were weakened; secondly, nationalism was strengthened; thirdly, the bipolar world of the superpowers undermined the world roles of the colonial powers.

b) Why were some European powers more prepared to decolonise than others?

Decolonisation was an uneven process through which some powers were more prepared to decolonise than others. The British were most prepared to decolonise after 1945 but only in those parts of the empire where preparations for self-government had been in hand during the inter-war period. Elsewhere, further investment in empire took place and the British were only persuaded to leave by a combination of rising nationalism, international pressure and economic considerations. The French and the Dutch were more reluctant decolonisers, considering their empires indispensable parts of their post-war economic recovery. The French particularly had a strong ideological commitment to empire. By contrast, the Belgians were the swiftest leavers, being unprepared to make the sustained military commitment necessary to cling on to the Congo. The Portuguese made the opposite decision, but it still resulted in an identical outcome, if delayed by over a decade.

c) Why were some decolonisations more violent than others?

The most violent decolonisations were those of the French and the Portuguese. Prime responsibility for this must lie with the obduracy of the metropoles. Militarism could easily come to the fore in a dictatorship like Portugal, but also did so temporarily in a fragile democracy like France. In both Algeria and Angola serious internecine conflict also occurred. Colonial wars have left a legacy of post-colonial violence in both. Superpower rivalries were responsible for much fighting in Angola and Mozambique, and in French Indo-China before that.

d) What economic considerations were at stake over decolonisation?

The 'economic calculus' has to take account of the fact that some colonies were more profitable than others. This means that there could have been no universal economic cause of decolonisation. Nevertheless, the arguments for European reorientation are strong. But no government, or group of 'gentlemanly capitalists' for that matter, sat down in smoke-filled rooms and planned decolonisation meticulously like accountants. Contingencies such as nationalist revolts or superpower interventions sometimes forced their hands. Overall, Simon Smith's judgement about Britain is sound and can be generalised:

> the underlying pragmatism rarely wavered. Britain pursued her imperial path not out of a sense of altruism, or even primarily out of concern for indigenous peoples, but for profit, whether in economic, political or military terms.[4]

e) How did the Cold War affect decolonisation?

The Cold War's grip upon decolonisation tightened through the period 1945–80. As early as 1946–54 we see American power conflicting with Soviet and Chinese in Indo-China. From then onwards there is hardly a decolonisation where superpower interests do not feature to a greater or lesser degree. Some analysts have concluded that by the 1960s wars of decolonisation were often Cold War surrogates. Thus, it is essential to see decolonisation as a process whose character was increasingly shaped by the world order in which it was played out. Its expectations may have been infinite, but its possibilities were limited.

3 Consequences

African poverty at the beginning of the twenty-first century plagues the world's conscience. A recent survey found that the average African is poorer than at the time of decolonisation. The continent's total output is just above that of Belgium. Its income distribution and access to essential services are as unequal as anywhere in the world. Outside South Africa, it has fewer roads than Poland. It has klepto-cratic (corruptly thieving) governments and raging civil wars, massive debts it can never repay, and a declining share of world trade.[5] It has the highest Aids infection rate of any continent, made worse by refugee migrants crossing non-existent state frontiers.

African cinema has left a film history of this post-colonial decline. Flora Gomes' film *The Blue Eyes of Yonta* (1991) is set in the former Portuguese colony of Guinea-Bissau in West Africa. It is a love story but also a lament for the failure of decolonisation to realise its ideals. Yonta's lover Vicente, once a revolutionary but now a struggling fish wholesaler, complains that his business is doomed by the frequent electricity failures that threaten his refrigerators. Yonta's reply is an eloquent echo of what Ferro has termed 'decolonization halted':[6]

> We can respect the past, but we cannot live in it. What we fought for has only been for some, when we thought it would be for all.

Zola Maseko's short film *The Foreigner* (1997) is set in Mozambique. It deals with one consequence of post-colonial poverty: migration. The street urchin Vusi befriends a new trader in the local market who gives him some clothes. 'The Foreigner' is resented by other traders because he is suspected of being a migrant from Zaire or Zambia. The next morning Vusi witnesses a murderous attack upon 'The Foreigner'. He recalls his wise words of the previous night warning of the calamity that African is turning against African, 'Ignorance will kill us all'.

Yet, growing impoverishment has not been the universal result of decolonisation because parts of Asia have progressed, notably those Pacific Rim states like Malaysia and Singapore that have been the objects of multinational investment. India sustains the world's largest democracy but also a demographic problem that Hobsbawm identifies as one of the two greatest the world faces (the other being ecologi-cal).[7] Africa's plight is partly explained by the lateness of its decoloni-sation for which it was insufficiently prepared, but also by historical conditions since decolonisation. Agrarian backwardness, the lack of prerequisites needed for industrialisation, under-investment by and indebtedness to the developed world have produced weak states vulnerable to corrupt government and the militarisation of politics.

And what of the former colonial powers in Europe? To borrow a phrase from Harold Macmillan, they have never had it so good.

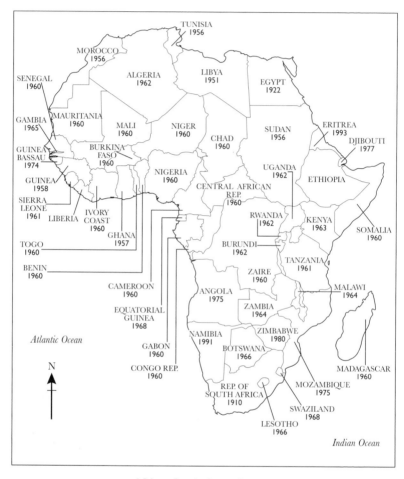

Africa after independence

References

1   Ferro, *Colonization*, p.350.
2   Darwin, *Britain and Decolonisation*, p.20.
3   Gifford and Louis, *Decolonization and African Independence*, p.xxvii.
4   Simon C. Smith, *British Imperialism 1750–1970* (Cambridge University Press, 1998), p.121.
5   Charlotte Denny, *The Guardian*, 15 June 2000.
6   Ferro, *Colonization*, p.344.
7   Hobsbawm, *Age of Extremes*, p.345.

Summary Diagram
The Causes of Decolonisation

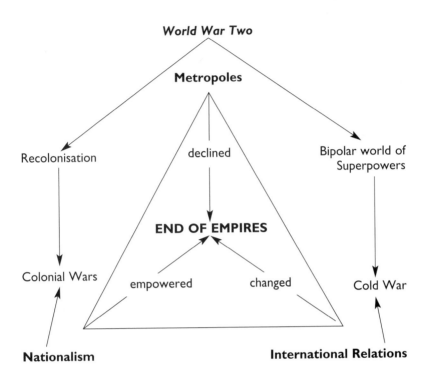

World War Two

Metropoles

Recolonisation

declined

Bipolar world of
Superpowers

END OF EMPIRES

Colonial Wars

empowered   changed

Cold War

Nationalism

International Relations

These questions should be used to test your understanding of the
whole book, not just the conclusions in Chapter 6. They are typical of
the type of broad, comparative questions asked by the main examining boards. You will usually be asked to base your answer on at least
two colonial powers.

1 To what extent was decolonisation in Asia and Africa a direct result of
   the Second World War?
2 Consider the view that decolonisation was more the initiative of the
   colonisers than the colonised.
3 'The decolonisation of Africa has been disastrous because it was prema-
   ture and badly managed'. Discuss.

Hints and Advice

1   Ask whether there were other causes that predate the War. Consider whether the later decolonisations can be called 'direct results'. Were there intervening causes? Evaluate all causes to address 'to what extent'.

2   Build upon the triangular diagram at the end of this chapter to decide whether it was declining metropoles or nationalism that was more responsible. Consider the effects of changing international relations, too.

3   This is a question about consequences. Do not bring in Asian examples, but consider whether all the colonial powers in Africa left a poor economic and political legacy, or only some. Distinguish also between colonies' readiness for decolonisation in terms of levels of development.

Further Reading

1 General

Raymond Betts, *Decolonization* (Routledge, 1998) is substantially concerned with the consequences of decolonisation in helping shape the modern world. **M.E. Chamberlain**, *Decolonization: the fall of the European Empires* (Blackwell, 1985) is a short, introductory study that concentrates heavily upon the British case, with an up-to-date bibliography. More substantial is **Marc Ferro**, *Colonization: A Global History* (Routledge, 1997), raising important questions about the limits of decolonisation as an historical process within a global economy. **Prosser Gifford** and **William Roger Louis** (editors), *Decolonization and African Independence: The Transfers of Power, 1960–1980* (Yale University Press, 1988) is a scholarly collection of essays from international experts, some African, on both general themes and specific areas. **Henri Grimal**, *Decolonization: the British, French, Dutch and Belgian Empires 1919–1963* (Routledge, 1978), originally published in French in 1963, shows its age by seeing nationalism as the main cause of decolonisation. It remains valuable for its great detail and its wealth of documentary sources. **J.K. Hargreaves**, *Decolonization in Africa* (Longman, 1988) contrasts the different patterns across the continent. **R.F. Holland**, *European Decolonization 1918–81* (Macmillan, 1985) contains challenging interpretative arguments, although it prioritises British discussion above others. **Paul Kennedy**, *The Rise and Fall of the Great Powers: Economic Change and Military Conflict 1500–2000* (Unwin Hyman, 1988) contains a grand theory of why empires fall due to over-extending themselves. **Bernard Waites**, *Europe and the Third World: from Colonialism to Decolonisation, c.1500–1998* (Macmillan, 1999) provides a scholarly, long-term context to decolonisation.

2 British Decolonisation

P.J. Cain and **A.G. Hopkins**, *British Imperialism: Crisis and Deconstruction 1914–1990* (Longman, 1993) is the second of two major volumes. **John Darwin**, *Britain and Decolonisation: the retreat from empire in the post-war world* (Macmillan, 1988) situates decolonisation within changing international relations after 1945. **John Darwin**, *The End of the British Empire: The Historical Debate* (Blackwell, 1991) is the best short introduction available to the historiography. **Simon C. Smith**, *British Imperialism 1750–1970* (Cambridge University Press, 1998) provides concise long-term context with good primary-source, documentary support. **Nicholas J. White**, *Decolonisation: The British Experience Since 1945* (Longman, 1999), places Britain within its European context and compares historians' perspectives.

Useful articles include the following. **Anthony Kirk-Greene**, 'Decolonisation in British Africa', *History Today*, January 1992, surveys recent historiography on this topic. **Peter Clements**, 'Legacies of Empire', *History Today*, April 1998, updates this in some respects. **Peter Heehs**, 'India's Divided Loyalties', *History Today*, July 1995, looks at the Indian National Army during the Second World War.

3 French Decolonisation

Raymond F. Betts, *France and Decolonisation 1900–1960* (Macmillan, 1991) is the best short study available. **Raymond F. Betts**, *Uncertain Dimensions: Western Overseas Empires in the Twentieth Century* (Oxford, 1985) is chiefly concerned to compare French with British experience.

Two articles by **Martin Evans** are valuable. 'French Resistance and the Algerian War', *History Today*, July 1991, examines French support for the FLN. 'Algeria: Thirty Years On', *History Today*, July 1992, examines the rise and decline of the FLN. **Gillian Staerck**, 'The Vietnam Revolution', *Modern History Review*, vol.10. no.2, Nov.1998, is a brief summary.

4 Dutch, Belgian and Portuguese Decolonisation

Petra M.H. Groen, 'Militant Response: The Dutch Use of Military Force and the Decolonization of the Dutch East Indies, 1945–60', *Journal of Imperial and Commonwealth History*, vol. XXI, Sept. 1993, No.3, is a rare account of the Dutch case in English. **Gillian Staerck**, 'Indonesia 1945–49', *Modern History Review*, vol.10, no.3, Feb. 1999, is a brief summary. On Belgium, **Jean-Philippe Peemans**, 'Imperial Hangovers: Belgium – the Economics of Decolonization', *Journal of Contemporary History*, XV, 1980, fills a gap. Portuguese decolonisation is better served. **W.G. Clarence-Smith**, *The Third Portuguese Empire, 1825–1975* (Manchester University Press, 1985) provides the long-term context. **Norrie MacQueen**, *The Decolonization of Portuguese Africa: Metropolitan Revolution and the Dissolution of Empire* (Longman, 1997) is the best single book on the Portuguese case, however. **Malyn Newitt**, *Portugal in Africa: The Last Hundred Years* (Hurst, 1981) is also useful.

Index